Aldous Huxley

Brave New World

Annotations
and Study Aids

by Rudolph F. Rau

Ernst Klett Schulbuchverlag

Contents

Introduction

What irony that Huxley never considered *Brave New World* to be his best novel, and yet it has become his most enduring one, with his other eight now largely unknown to the general reading public. It was written as a light-hearted satire of H.G. Wells' *Men Like Gods*. We may ask why this novel, written more than half a century ago, has still remained so appealing. In part we can ascribe its popularity to Huxley's acerbic wit and his use of all the satiric tricks of the literary trade. It may be also his dealing with the core problems of 20th century Western society, some of which have made us increasingly uncomfortable. We need only think of the very possibility of hand-tailoring human beings by means of genetic manipulation.

While reading *Brave New World* in itself can be an enjoyable experience, some aspects of the novel can be better appreciated if one knows something of his other novels, especially two written before *Brave New World* and his last novel written shortly before his death in 1963.

Antic Hay (1923) satirizes the vacuous life style of Britain's upper class after World War One; the novel anticipates *Brave New World's* satiric treatment of loveless sex and mindless cultural activities.[1] Huxley's novel *Point Counter Point* (1928) reveals the influence of the English writer D.H. Lawrence (1885-1930). A character in the novel, Rampion, espouses Lawrence's ideal of a balance between "…reason, feeling, instinct, the life of the body." Rampion (Lawrence in disguise) takes a skeptical stance towards science, industry and progress – much as Jean-Jacques Rousseau did in the 18th century. Lawrence lived in New Mexico for a short time, and was fascinated by the Pueblo Indians (Huxley got much of his information about them from him). Typical of Huxley: while agreeing with much of what Rousseau and Lawrence said, they too fall under the satiric axe in the form of the Savage and the Reservation.

Huxley's last novel (1962) *Island* outlines his idea of an ideal society that is strikingly like the Brave New World society he seemingly rejected earlier. There is practically no literature, mind expanding drugs are used, there is an educational system that includes conditioning and hypnosis. Huxley envisions a society of loose "voluntary families" and a liberal sexuality. But his society is free of violence and commercialism, and is in harmony with both technology and nature.

Being the upper class British intellectual that he was (having enjoyed a first-rate education at Eton and Oxford) he was aware of the sum total of Western culture, be it science or literature: he was the 20th century Renaissance Man. Indeed it was rumoured that he had committed the entire Encyclopedia Britannica to memory. Understandably, it is beyond the scope of this reading guide to deal in depth with all the themes and allusions in *Brave New World*. Alone dealing with all the theological ramifications of Huxley's novel would fill volumes. Those aspects of the novel most relevant to the needs of students in a German *Oberstufe* have been given attention. Even so, the background material offered here is more than any class will be able to deal with in the available time, and teachers will therefore need to choose what suits their particular classes.

The reader is strongly advised to read the novel first before attempting to read the Foreword Huxley wrote 14 years after *Brave New World* was published. It gives his "second thoughts" on some aspects of the novel.

2 **enduring** lasting, still able to exist – 6 **to ascribe** to consider that s.th. is caused by a certain factor, to attribute s.th. to a factor – **acerbic** [əˈsɜːbɪk] sharp, biting – 8 **core** central, most important – 10 **to hand-tailor** (usu. said of clothing) here: to make s.th. to certain specifications – 17 **vacuous** [ˈvækjʊəs] empty, without any meaning – 18 **to anticipate** to do s.th. in advance of s.th. else – 22 **to espouse** [ɪˈspaʊz] to give support to a certain ideal or cause – 24 **stance** attitude – 25 **Rousseau** French philosopher (1718-1778) – 35 **to envision** to think of as possible, to foresee – 40 **Renaissance Man** [rɪˈneɪsns] a person who has wide interests and is experienced in many areas, such as was typical during the Renaissance – 43 **scope** the intended area to be covered – 45 **ramification** additional consequence that makes a topic more complicated

Annotations and Chapter Questions

The following abbreviations are used:

arch.	archaic	Fr.	French	opp.	opposite
bibl.	biblical	Ger.	German	p./pp.	page(s)
ch./chs.	chapter(s)	i.e.	that is	pl.	plural
cf.	compare	It.	Italian	relig.	religious
coll.	colloquial	l./ll.	line(s)	s.o.	someone
derog.	derogatory	Lat.	Latin	Span.	Spanish
e.g.	for example	lit.	literary	s.th.	something
esp.	especially	mus.	musical	theol.	theological
etc.	et cetera	n.	noun	usu.	usually
fig.	figurative	o.s.	oneself	v.	verb
form.	formal				

BNW = Brave New World
EJL = information from Edmund J. Ladd, Curator of Ethnology at the Museum of New Mexico, Santa Fe

5 = page numbers of the Grafton/Klett edition
5 = page numbers of the old Grafton/ELT edition

3	**brave**	here: wonderful	*3*
	Brave New World	The title of the novel comes from act V, scene i of Shakespeare's play *The Tempest*. Miranda, who has lived most of her life on a magic island with her banished father, says to visitors from the outside world: "Oh brave new world, That hath such people in't!"	
5	**Les utopies … plus libre.**	translation: "It seems that utopias are indeed more realizable than was previously thought. We now find ourselves faced with a question that is quite worrying in another way: How do we avoid their eventual realization? … Life is advancing towards utopias. And perhaps a new age is beginning, an age when intellectuals and the cultivated class will think about ways of avoiding utopias and returning to a society that is not a utopia, less pefect and more free."	*5*
	Nicolas Berdiaeff	(also spelled Nicholas Berdyev, 1874–1948) Russian theologian and philosopher, who in his youth was a Marxist. He later rejected Marxism in favour of a more religious view of life. He was especially concerned about the negative effects of modern technology on man, and the theological question of the freedom of will. He was expelled from the Soviet Union in 1922.	

squat [skwɒt]	short and thick in an unattractive way
hatchery	a place where eggs are artificially prepared to produce animals
to condition	to manipulate s. o. so that this person permanently behaves in a certain way. First experiments with conditioning were made by Ivan Pavlov (1849–1936), and continued by J. B. Watson (1878–1958) and B. F. Skinner (1904–1990).
shield	here: large sign
Community, Identity, Stability	an allusion to the slogan of the French Revolution: Liberté! Egalité! Fraternité! (Liberty! Equality! Brotherhood!)
for all ...	in spite of
pane	a sheet of glass in a window
harsh	unpleasant, too bright
to glare	to shine with a very bright light that is difficult to look at
draped	covered with a cloth
lay figure	a model of the human body that can be put in any position, used by artists
pallid ['--]	pale
academic	associated with an art academy
goose-flesh	condition of the skin when it is exposed to the cold; here: an unclothed human body used as a model
bleakly	coldy, dismally, cheerlessly
porcelain ['pɔ:səlɪn]	Porzellan
wintriness	lack of warmth (as in winter), cheerlessness
to respond to	to react to
overalls	working clothes
gloved	in gloves
corpse-coloured	like the colour of a dead body
barrel	the tube-like part of a microscope that contains the lenses
streak	a long thin mark *(Streifen)*
luscious ['lʌʃəs]	very pleasant, extremely attractive to the senses
in long recession	a long distance to the back
to fertilize ['---]	to cause a male sperm to join a female egg
to plunge [plʌndʒ]	to throw (s. o./o. s.) completely into an activity, to become totally involved in s. th.
absent-minded	not paying attention to one's surroundings
to soliloquize [sə'lɪləkwaɪz]	usu.: to speak to o. s. as if alone
hum	the sound of singing with closed lips *(Summen)*
absorbed	completely interested
callow	with very little experience
abjectly	lacking all pride or self-respect
heel	back part of the foot or shoe

20	**to scribble**	to write quickly and carelessly
	straight from the horse's mouth	direct from the source (from the idea that the only reliable way to know the age of a horse is to look at the teeth in its mouth)
	to make a point of doing s. th.	to do s. th. very deliberately
	particulars	details, practical facts 16
	virtue	goodness *(Tugendhaftigkeit)*
	generalities	general ideas, abstractions
	evil	s. th. which is bad or not desirable
	fret-sawyer	s. o. who uses a fret-saw (as a hobby), which is a small saw for cutting designs in wood
	menacing ['---]	threatening
	geniality [ˌdʒiːnɪ'ælətɪ]	friendliness
	to settle down to s. th.	to start to do s. th.
	prominent	sticking out *(vorstehend)*
	florid ['flɒrɪd]	like a flower (in shape or colour)
	A. F.	= after Ford. Instead of using A. D. (Anno Domini) this society uses A. F. in memory of Henry Ford (1863–1947), who was the first to successfully mass produce the automobile. A. F. 632 would be about 500 years from now.
	it didn't occur to you	you didn't think of …
	zealous ['zeləs]	eager *(eifrig)*
	incubator ['ɪnkjʊbeɪtə]	a box-like device that keeps eggs warm until the young animal hatches; also used (in our society) for premature babies
	insulated	with special protection against outside temperatures
	rack	a frame or shelf for holding things
	racks upon racks	a great number of racks
	test-tube	narrow glass container used in laboratories *(Reagenzglas)*
	ova ['əʊvə]	pl. of *ovum,* female egg cell
	gamete ['gæmiːt]	a sex cell (sperm) ready to join with another cell (ovum) to form a new individual
	ram	male sheep
21	**thermogene**	special orange-coloured insulating material used to keep parts of the body warm
	to beget [-'-]	to be the father of
	to scurry	to hurry
	illegible [-'---]	difficult to read
	surgical	by means of an operation (as has now – since the late 70s – become common practice as a treatment for infertility)
	to undergo	to go through s. th., to experience s. th.
	account	here: explanation, report, description
	to excise [ek'saɪz]	to remove by cutting out
	ovary ['əʊvərɪ]	female organ that creates the ova (eggs)
	salinity	amount of salt in a liquid
	viscosity [-'---]	thickness *(Zähflüssigkeit)*

	liquor ['lɪkə]	liquid	
	to detach	to separate	
	to ripen	to develop and become mature	
	charge	here: a person s. o. is responsible for	
	to draw off	to carefully remove a liquid from s. th.	
	slide	a thin piece of glass to put an object on and then place under a microscope	
	porous ['pɔ:rəs]	with a structure that allows liquids to pass through slowly	*17*
	receptacle	container	
	to immerse [-'-]	to put into a liquid	
	bouillon ['bu:jɒn]	(Fr.) a clear soup	
	spermatozoa [ˌ---'--]	male sex cells ready to fertilize	
	Alphas, etc.	The first five letters of the Greek alphabet are used to label the castes or social classes of this society.	
	to bottle	to put in a bottle	
	Bokanovsky	fictitious name; may have been suggested by Ivan Vassilevich Bokanovsky, Russian revolutionary	
22	**to bud**	to develop like the buds of a plant *(knospen, keimen)*	
	to proliferate [-'---]	to increase rapidly in numbers	
	to arrest	to bring to a stop	
	to check	to stop	
	to emerge	to appear, come out	
	to purr	to make a low continuous sound, like a contented cat	
	X-ray	kind of radiation discovered by W. K. Roentgen in 1895	
	susceptible [-'---]	likely to be affected by s. th.	
	to chill	to lower the temperature of s. th. so it becomes cold	
	to dose [s]	to give a certain amount of drugs or medicine	
	consequently	after that	
	to burgeon ['bɜ:dʒən]	to grow rapidly, develop quickly	
	in a fair way	likely	
	prodigious [prə'dɪdʒəs]	very great, enormous	*18*
	piddling	small and unimportant	
	in the old viviparous days [vɪ'vɪpərəs]	i. e. when women gave birth to children in their own bodies	
	score	a group of twenty	
	to fling (flung, flung)	to throw out	
	largesse [-'-]	(Fr.) money and gifts to poor people	
23	**to wheel round on**	to quickly turn to	
	batch	the amount produced at one time	
	to staff	to provide with personnel	
	tremulous ['tremjʊləs]	trembling	
	alas [ə'læs]	unfortunately	
	to reach maturity [-'---]	to become fully grown	
	to dribble out	here: to produce in small quantities	

	Podsnap	probably an allusion to a self-satisfied character in Charles Dickens' *Our Mutual Friend* (1865)
	to accelerate	to increase the speed
24	**to yield**	to produce (a harvest) *19*
	to beckon	to make a sign with one's hand that s. o. should come closer
	ruddy	having a healthy reddish colour
	vivacious [vɪ'veɪʃəs]	lively
	to rattle on	to talk at length
	Mombasa [-'--]	a city in Kenya, Africa
	pituitary [pɪ'tjʊɪtərɪ]	here: an extract from the pituitary gland *(Hirnanhangdrüse)*
	combat ['--]	here: the desire to fight
	the lift of his chin was challenging	i. e. the way he lifted his chin showed he was ready to accept the challenge
	to decant [dɪ'kænt]	to pour a liquid (e. g. wine) from one container to another; here: to remove the fully developed baby from the test-tube
	in embryo	still in the embryo stage
	to clap	to hit with an open hand
	benefit	the advantages
	modestly	not wishing to boast *(bescheiden)*
	bustle	excited activity
	flap	*Lappen*
	sow [saʊ]	female pig
	peritoneum [--'---]	tissue surrounding the internal organs of the abdomen *(Bauchfell)*
25	**sub-basement**	a floor below the cellar
	hatch	small door
	Bottle-Liner	i. e. the worker whose job it is to put the flap of peritoneum into the bottle (to line = to cover the inside surface of s. th.)
	to smooth-down	to make flat
	interminable [-'----]	endless
	to matriculate [-'---]	to introduce into a "mother" (usu.: to become a student at a university)
	deftly	skilfully
	lining	i. e. the covering of peritoneum inside the test-tube
	to slit	to make a long narrow cut
	morula ['---]	the embryo at a very early stage of development
	saline solution ['seɪlaɪn]	salty liquid
	heredity [-'---]	*Vererbung, Abstammung*
	predestinaton [ˌpri:destɪ'neɪʃn]	the act of determining s.th. ahead of time; also: a belief in Calvinism that only certain people are saved by God and will enter heaven (verb: "to predestinate" [-'--] or "to predestine")
	card-index	a systematic listing of information on cards
	with relish	with enjoyment
26	**thickening twilight**	increasing darkness

	infiltration [ˌ--'--]	the act of secretly going into a place without being noticed	
	waggish	clever and amusing	
	in effect	in fact	
	sultry [ʌ]	unpleasantly hot and humid	
	crimson	deep red *(purpurrot)*	*21*
	to bulge [ʌ]	to swell, to be very full	
	to recede	to move back	
	tier [tɪə]	level	
	to glint	to shine brightly	
	innumerable [ɪ'nju:mərəbl]	a great number of	
	ruby ['ru:bɪ]	a red precious stone	
	dim	not easy to see because of the dark	
	spectre ['spektə]	ghost	
	lupus ['lu:pəs]	a disease that eats away the skin	
	with all the symptoms of lupus	i. e. appearing to have this illness (because of the red light)	
	hum and rattle	background noise *(Surren und Klappern)*	
	to stir	to move	
27	**spidery**	like the web woven by a spider	
	steelwork	steel construction	
	to fade away	to gradually disappear into the distance	
	demijohn	a large bottle with a short narrow neck often with handles at the neck	
	escalator ['--ˌ--]	moving staircase	
	conveyor	moving belt for transporting things around a factory	
	circuit ['sɜ:kɪt]	movement in a complete circle	
	duly	in a proper manner	
	surrogate ['---]	substitute	
	placentin	made-up word: extract from the placenta	
	thyroxin [θaɪ'rɒksɪ:n]	a hormone from the thyroid gland *(Schilddrüse)*	
	corpus luteum	a yellow mass of cells in the ovary formed after an ovum is released	
	jet	*Düse*	
	to administer [-'---]	to give	
	maternal [-'--]	having to do with a mother	*22*
	circulation [ˌsɜ:kjʊ'leɪʃn]	here: the movement of blood	
	reservoir	a large tank for storing s. th.	
	centrifugal [sen'trɪfjʊgl]	working on the basis of centrifugal force *(Fliehkraft)*	
28	**anaemia** [ə'ni:mɪə]	condition in which the blood has too few red cells	
	hog	male pig that has been castrated	
	foetal ['fi:tl]	having to do with a foetus [fi:təs] (the embryo after it has developed head, legs, and arms)	
	foal [fəʊl]	young horse	
	in consequence	as a result	
	familiarity [-ˌ--'---]	a certain amount of experience	
	gravity ['grævɪtɪ]	seriousness	

	trauma of decanting	a satiric allusion to the "trauma of birth". Otto Rank (1884–1937), a pupil of Freud, believed the shock of birth caused later mental problems.
	to enumerate [ɪ'nju:məreɪt]	to name things one by one
	precaution	an action to prevent future problems
	in the neighbourhood of	near
	freemartin	usu.: a sterile cow; here: a female person who is sterile
	ground	here: background
	nuisance ['nju:səns]	something that annoys, bothers
	margin of safety	more safety than the minimum necessary
	realm [relm]	area
	mere	simple
	slavish	like a slave; here: unoriginal
	to content oneself with s. th.	to be satisfied with s. th.
	to hatch out	to cause to be born
29	**sewage worker** ['sju:ɪdʒ]	a person who deals with waste matter from houses and factories
	World Controller	the head of this society
	to acknowledge	to show that one has heard or received s. th.
	spanner	tool for tightening or loosening screws *(Schraubenschlüssel)*
	fraction	very small amount
	nut	*Schraubenmutter*
	revolution counter	an instrument that counts the number of times s. th. turns
	pace	step
	shortage	not enough of the amount needed
	below par	below the accepted standard
	ingenuous [ɪn'dʒenjʊəs]	naive
	ass	foolish person (literally: a donkey)
	dwarf	an abnormally small person
	confidential [ˌ--'--]	as if telling a secret
	eager	keen, wanting very much to do s. th.
30	**maturation**	the process of becoming mature
	benefaction [--'--]	good deed, benefit
	hence	therefore
	fruit	here: result
	justly	quite properly
	superfluous [su:'pɜ:flʊəs]	not needed or wanted
	immaturity [ˌ--'---]	state of not being mature
	infectious [ɪn'fekʃəs]	tending to spread from one person to another *24*
	endocrine ['endəʊˌkraɪn]	of the glands that secrete internally, e. g. the thyroid *(Schilddrüse),* adrenal glands *(Nebennieren)*

	to postulate [ˈpɒstjʊleɪt]	to make up a theory to explain s. th.	
	germinal [ˈdʒɜːmɪnl]	happening at the earliest stage of development	
	to account for	to explain	
	to revert [-ˈ-]	to return	
	all but solved	very nearly solved	
	to sigh [saɪ]	*seufzen*	
31	**to alternate** [ˈ--ˌ-]	to happen by turns, first one then the other	
	to wed to	here: to unite or combine with (usu.: to get married)	
	acetate silk [ˈæsɪteɪt]	a synthetic textile	
	to endorse	to support	
	to thrive	to develop well	
	sententiously [-ˈ---]	in a way that seems very wise	
	delicately	with a great deal of care and skill	
	to probe	to examine with a long thin instrument	
	syringe [sɪˈrɪndʒ]	a medical instrument with a long thin needle used to inject or remove liquids	
	gelatinous [dʒəˈlætɪnəs]	jelly-like	
	Lenina	seems to be formed from Lenin, the adopted name of the Russian revolutionary Vladimir Ilyich Ulyanov (1870–1924)	
	to withdraw	to remove, take back	*25*
	with a start	with a sudden movement of surprise	
	… the lupus and the purple eyes …	ironic: actually an effect of the crimson light	
	to flash	to shine (fig.)	
	pat	a gentle tap, a light stroke with the open hand to show friendliness (rather patronizing)	
	deferential [ˌdefəˈrenʃl]	showing respect because of the other person's higher position	
32	**typhoid** [ˈtaɪfɔɪd]	typhoid fever *(Typhus)*	
	sleeping sickness	a serious illness in Africa caused by the tsetse fly	
	to inoculate [ɪˈnɒkjʊleɪt]	to protect s. o. against a disease by introducing into the body a small amount of what causes the disease	
	gill [g]	organs through which fish (and embryos) breathe *(Kieme)*	
	lead [led]	a heavy metal, the chemical element Pb *(Blei)*	
	caustic soda	a chemical compound, NaOH *(Ätznatron)*	
	tar	a black, sticky substance used for road surfaces	
	chlorine [ˈklɔːriːn]	the chemical element Cl *(Chlor)*	
	ticklish	delicate, difficult	
	to slacken off	to make slower	
	topsy-turvydom	situation where everything is "topsy-turvy" i. e. the opposite of what is normal	
33	**nursery**	a room where small children are cared for	*26*
	Decanting Room	this society's equivalent of Delivery Room *(Kreißsaal)*	
	indulgently	allowing s. o. a special favour	

1. Describe the setting of the novel. Say what you now know of
   a) the time,
   b) the place, and
   c) the historical background.
2. What is the dominant tone of this chapter? How is it created?
3. Describe the reproduction technology of this society. Compare it with what you know of actual scientific developments
   a) at the time the novel was written;
   b) today.
4. Consider the sex-roles of the characters that have been presented so far. How do they relate to Huxley's own time? How appropriate are they in Brave New World society?

34 **Chapter Two** *27*

DHC	Director of Hatcheries and Conditioning
Pavlovian [-'---]	referring to the Russian physiologist Ivan Pavlov (1849–1936). He was especially famous for his experiments with animals in which he discovered conditioned reflexes.
bare	with no furniture
regulation	according to the rules of the government
viscose	textile made by a special treatment of cellulose
linen ['lɪnən]	a natural fibre made from flax
aseptically [ˌeɪ'septɪklɪ]	so as to prevent any infections
to be engaged in	to be busy doing s. th.
blossom	(usu. blossoms) flowers
petal ['petl]	colourful part of a flower *(Blütenblatt)*
ripe-blown	full-blown and ripe *(prall)*
cherub ['tʃerəb]	angel depicted in the form of a child *(Putte)*
Aryan ['eərɪən]	here: of the racial type common in Europe. The term was popularized in Nazi Germany in order to distinguish the "native" Europeans (Nordic, Celtic and other sub-groups) from other white Caucasians (e.g. Semites). *(arisch)*
luminous ['lu:mɪnəs]	bright, clear
apoplectic [ˌæpə'plektɪk]	very excited and red in the face
celestial [sɪ'lestɪəl]	heavenly
blowing trumpets	a continuation of the ironic metaphor of the cherub, who is often seen in paintings and baroque churches blowing a trumpet
posthumous ['pɒstjʊməs]	after death
marble	a hard, polished stone often used decoratively in churches, palaces, etc. *(Marmor)*
to stiffen to attention	to stand up straight like a soldier coming to attention
curt	abrupt, short, not in a polite way
quarto	a book of large size

	dumb-waiter	usu. a stand with shelves usually used to hold food about to be served
	laden ['leɪdn]	loaded
	wire-netted	made of wire formed into a net *(aus Maschendraht)*
35	**evident**	obvious
	khaki ['kɑ:kɪ]	(cloth with a) yellow-brown colour
	to crawl	to move forward on one's hands and knees
	cluster	a number of things of the same kind close together
	sleek	smooth and shining
	momentary	only for a short time *28*
	eclipse [ɪ'klɪps]	usu.: the obscuring of the sun by the moon, or of the moon by the earth's shadow *(Finsternis)*
	profound	deep
	to suffuse [sə'fju:z]	to completely spread over and become part of s. th.
	rank	row
	squeal	a long high cry, like that of a pig
	gurgle	sound made back in the throat
	twitter	sound like that made by birds
	swift	fast
	transfigured	changed into s. th. beautiful *(verklärt)*
	to crumple	to press together
	illuminated [-'----]	filled with light
	switchboard	board containing the controls *(Schalttafel)*
	lever ['li:və]	*Hebel*
	to shriek [i:]	to make a wild high cry
	to start	to make a sudden movement because of a shock
	to distort	to twist out of the normal shape
	deafening ['defənɪŋ]	extremely loud
	to proceed to do s. th.	to continue with another action
	to rub in	here: to make sure the lesson is properly learnt
36	**insane**	mad
	spasmodic [-'--]	happening for short periods of time at irregular intervals
	yelp	a short sudden cry of pain
	to twitch	to make sudden little movements that can't be controlled
	limbs	arms and legs
	jerkily	(moving) suddenly and abruptly
	tug	a quick and strong pull
	to bawl [bɔ:l]	to shout loudly and harshly
	to cease	to stop
	sob	*Schluchzen*
	maniac ['meɪnɪæk]	mad person
	howl	long loud cry of fear or pain
	pussy	cat } examples of "baby-talk"; all these expressions are contained in English nursery rhymes *(Kinderreime)*
	cock-a-doodle-doo	cock
	baa-baa black sheep	
	to shrink (shrank, shrunk)	to move away from s. th. because of fright or dislike

	volume ['vɒlju:m]	how loud s. th. is	*29*
	compromisingly	suggestively	
	indissolubly [ˌɪndɪ'sɒljʊblɪ]	unbreakably	
	to put asunder	to separate	
	What man has … asunder.	bibl. allusion referring to Matthew 19:6 where Christ talks about the bonds of marriage: "What therefore God hath joined together, let not man put asunder."	
	unalterable [ˌʌn'ɔ:ltərəbl]	unchangeable	
37	**to decondition**	to undo the conditioning	
	on grounds of	because of	
	or thereabouts	approximately, roughly	
	to consume	i. e. to make use of and pay for it	
	primrose	a small yellow spring flower *(Primel)*	
	grave	serious	
	gratuitous [grə'tju:ɪtəs]	offered without expecting any payment	
	at any rate	at least	
	sound	valid, logical	*30*
	to entail [-'-]	to require	
38	**to clear one's throat**	to give a small cough before speaking *(sich räuspern)*	
	once upon a time	*es war einmal …*	
	Our Ford	an allusion to "Our Lord", i. e. Jesus Christ (see note on "A. F.", p. 20/*16*)	
	Reuben	a name common among Jews (in the Bible, Reuben was Jacob's eldest son, the ancestor of one of the tribes of Israel; Genesis 29:32)	
	officious [ə'fɪʃəs]	a bit too willing to give advice or help	
	to show off	to try to impress others with one's ability	
	to blush	to become red in the face with shame	
	to draw a distinction	to recognize the difference	
	smut	obscene words or pictures	
	to rub in	to emphasize s. th. so that it won't be forgotten	
	by an oversight	as the result of a careless mistake	
39	**crash, crash!**	sign of the students' embarrassment at hearing the words "mother" and "father"	
	gross [grəʊs]	unpleasant, vulgar	
	crash and crash	i. e. mother and father	*31*
	to venture	to risk doing s. th.	
	lecture	formal talk *(Vortrag)*	
	curious	strange, unusual	
	have been permitted to come down to us	i. e. can still be read by us	
	George Bernard Shaw	(1856–1950) born in Dublin, considered the greatest dramatist writing in English since Shakespeare. Although his plays focus on ideas (e.g. criticism of the British class system and religion), he used language in a brilliant and witty way.	
	well-authenticated [ɔ:'θentɪkeɪtɪd]	well proven	

	wink	opening and shutting one's eye very quickly as a signal to someone that s. th. is a joke or a secret
	snigger	laughing quietly without respect, usu. at s. th. felt to be obscene *(Kichern)*
	wink and snigger	i. e. mother and father (see above: "crash", etc.)
	incomprehensible [ɪnˌkɒmprɪˈhensəbl]	impossible to understand
	discourse [ˈ--]	a serious talk
	hypnopaedia [ˌhɪpnəʊˈpiːdɪə]	learning during sleep
	to elapse	to pass, to go by
	T-Model	Henry Ford's extremely successful mass-produced car, of which over 15 million were sold from 1908 to 1928.
	a sign of the T	cf. the Christian "sign of the cross"
	reverently [ˈrevərəntlɪ]	showing a great deal of respect
	to follow suit	to do the same thing as s. o. else
	furiously	here: at great speed (usu.: angrily)
40	**on the wrong track**	mistaken, seeking the wrong goal
	limply	loosely, not stiffly
	grating [ˈɡreɪtɪŋ]	opening covered partly by metal or wire *(Gitter)*
	to fall short of	to fail to reach
	basin [ˈbeɪsn]	area from which a river gets its water
	to extend	to reach, to stretch
	degrees of latitude	degrees north or south of the equator *(Breitengrade)*
	investigator [-ˈ----]	researcher *32*
	to abandon	to give up, to discontinue
41	**indefatigably** [ˌɪndɪˈfætɪɡəblɪ]	never becoming tired
	sibilant	making a hissing sound [s]
	categorical imperative [ˌ--ˈ---] [-ˈ---]	an allusion to the philosophy of Immanuel Kant (1724–1804) who first used this expression to mean the highest principle of morality against which all acts are to be tested (here: the command "Silence")
	to tiptoe	to walk quietly on one's toes
	threshold	line of a doorway dividing "in" from "out" *(Türschwelle)*
	shuttered	with the shutters *(Fensterladen)* of a window closed
	twilight	growing darkness
	dormitory	a large bedroom where several people sleep
	cot	a bed for a young child with bars round it so that the child cannot fall out
	murmur	a continuous low sound
	faint	very soft
	remotely	as if far away
	to come to attention	to stand up straight like a soldier
	elementary	basic
	class consciousness	being taught about one's social class and how good it is (cf. Marxism/British society)

	trumpet	here: loudspeaker	*33*
	to project [-ˈ-]	to stick out	
42	**beastly**	(upper-class usage) unpleasant	
	frightfully	awfully, very	
	thin ghost	i. e. the loudspeaker under the pillow	
	to mutter	to speak very quietly so that others can hardly understand what is being said	
	whiff	slight smell	
	asafoetida [ˌæsəˈfetɪdə]	a bitter and bad smelling substance obtained from the roots of several plants, formally used in medicine	
	crude	too simple, primitive	
	wholesale	done in great numbers without enough care	
	to bring home	to make s. o. clearly understand s. th.	
	to inculcate [ˈɪnkʌlkeɪt]	to fix ideas into s. o.'s mind by repetition	
	course	pattern, manner, way	
	insinuating [-ˈ----]	managing to get acceptance by using indirect methods	
43	**to wear holes**	to slowly make holes by erosion	*34*
	sealing-wax	wax used for sealing envelopes or documents *(Siegelwachs)*	
	to adhere	to stick	
	to incrust	to cover with a crust	
	to incorporate	to become a part of something larger	
	scarlet	deep red	
	blob	a soft mass	
	Oh, Ford	cf. our common exclamation "Oh, Lord"	

1. Find out what you can about Ivan Pavlov (see p. 34/27) and his experiments with animals. Also look up "Behaviorism", the school of psychology which the Americans Watson and Skinner developed from his findings. Discuss how these theories relate to Brave New World.
2. How does Huxley satirize consumerism and class structure?

44 **Chapter Three** *35*

to squat [skwɒt]	to sit on one's heels	
shrub	bush	
nightingale [ˈnaɪtɪŋgeɪl]	bird with a very sweet voice *(Nachtigall)*	
boskage [ˈbɒskɪdʒ]	thicket, a small group of bushes growing together	
to go out of tune	to start to sing notes that are slightly wrong	
lime tree	*Linde*	
drowsy [ˈdraʊzɪ]	sleepy	
bumble-puppy	usu.: a game in which a ball, attached by a string to a post, is hit so that the string winds round the post	
to revolve	to rotate	
to hurl	to throw with great force	

	aperture ['æpətʃə]	opening	
	to pierce	to cut a hole in s. th. with a sharp instrument	
	casing ['keɪsɪŋ]	outer metal covering *(Gehäuse)*	
	to muse [mju:z]	to say in a thoughtful way	
	netting	net	
	folly	stupidity	
	elaborate [ɪ'læbərət]	complicated	
	bay	here: small area of low ground	
	clump [klʌmp]	a small group of trees, flowers, etc.	
45	**heather** ['heðə]	flowering moorland plant *(Heidekraut)*	
	focussed ['fəʊkəst]	concentrated	
	intent on	having the firm intention to do s. th.	
	patronizing ['pætrənaɪzɪŋ]	with a superior manner, looking down on others	
	to put aside	to give up	
	contempt	dislike of s. th. regarded as inferior *(Verachtung)*	*36*
	maudlin ['mɔ:dlɪn]	foolishly sentimental	
	boo-hooing	crying	
	shrubbery	a number of shrubs planted together	
	to trot	to walk at a fast pace	
	reassuringly [ˌri:ə'ʃʊərɪŋ]	trying to make s. o. feel confident again	
	Trotsky	an allusion to Leon Trotsky (1879–1940), leading figure in the Russian Revolution. After a disagreement with Stalin, he was forced to leave Russia. In 1940 he was killed by an agent of Stalin's while living in exile in Mexico.	
46	**to scamper**	to hurry quickly	
	was lost to sight	disappeared	
	exquisite ['ekskwɪzɪt]	charming	
	to suppress	to prohibit	
	incredulity [ˌɪnkrɪ'dju:lətɪ]	lack of belief	
	adolescent [ˌ--'--]	teenager	*37*
	barring	except for	
	surreptitious [ˌsʌrəp'tɪʃəs]	done secretly	
	auto-erotism	(usu. eroticism) sexual activity without a partner	
	resonant ['rezənənt]	deep, loud and clear	
	startlingly	causing surprise	
	fringe	outer edge	
47	**scattered**	placed irregularly throughout the area	
	to dart	to move suddenly and quickly	
	effusive [ɪ'fju:sɪv]	showing pleasure or enthusiasm in an exaggerated way	
	his fordship	*BNW's* version of "His Lordship"	
	Mustapha ['mʊstəfə]	a Turkish name; possibly from Mustafa Kemal (1881–1938), Turkish general and statesman who tried to westernize the country	
	Mond [mɒnd]	possibly from Alfred Mond (1868–1930), founder of ICI, one of the largest chemical	

	industries in Great Britain; he tried to improve the conditions of the working class
discarnate [-'--]	having no physical body
trumpet mouth	i. e. loudspeaker
shift	one of the working periods into which a day is divided
… off duty	here: … must now stop working
pointedly	done on purpose
Bernard	possibly an allusion to the playwright, George Bernard Shaw (see notes on p. 39/*31*) and/or the French physiologist Claude Bernard (1813–1883)
Marx	an (ironic) allusion to Karl Marx (1818–1883), German philosopher and founder of communism
to avert oneself	to turn away from
unsavoury [ˌʌn'seɪvərɪ]	distasteful, unpleasant, disagreeable
to give place to	to be replaced by
Crowne	possibly an allusion to John Crowne (1640–1703), English dramatist; either because of his hedonistic views, or because he wrote plays that were second-rate *38*
to pop out	to jump out
resident	here: local representative of a higher power
48 **shrimp**	small, lobster-like sea animal *(Krabbe, Garnele)*
bunk	nonsense
History is bunk.	In an interview in the *Chicago Tribune,* (1916), the real Henry Ford (1863–1947) said: "History is more or less bunk."
whisk	a small brush to remove dust
Harappa [hə'ræpə]	an ancient city in Pakistan where the Indus civilization once flourished
Ur of the Chaldees [ɜː] [kæl'diːz]	an important center of Sumerian culture located in Mesopotamia, also the home of Abraham.
Thebes [θiːbz]	an ancient city in Greece, also an ancient city in Egypt
Babylon ['bæbɪlən]	chief city of ancient Mesopotamia
Cnossos ['knɒsəs]	an ancient city in Crete
Mycenae [maɪ'siːniː]	ancient Greek city
Odysseus [ə'dɪsɪəs]	hero of the epic by the Greek poet Homer (800 B.C.)
Job [dʒəʊb]	character in the Old Testament *(Hiob)*
Gotama [-'--]	another name for Buddha
speck	a small piece of s. th.
Middle Kingdom	the Chinese empire
King Lear	a tragedy by Shakespeare about an old man and his three daughters
(Blaise) **Pascal**	(1623–1662) French philosopher, mathematician, and physicist
Passion ['pæʃən]	here: a musical composition based on Christ's final suffering (e. g. Bach's *St Matthew Passion)*

	Requiem ['rekwɪˌem]	a musical piece mourning s. o.'s death (e. g. that by Mozart or Verdi)	
	feely	cf. "movie", "talkie"	
	Alhambra [æl'hæmbrə]	popular name for a cinema (taken from a palace built by the Moors in Spain in the 13th and 14th centuries)	
	rug	small carpet	
	… on a bearskin rug	a cliché deriving from the novel *Three Weeks* by Elinor Glyn. Its erotic scenes on a tiger-skin caused quite a scandal in its time (1907).	
	tactual ['tæktjʊəl]	having to do with the sense of touch	
49	**rumour**	information spread round that may or may not be true	*39*
	Ford knew …	cf. "God knows …" or "God knew …"	
	to intercept	here: to notice and react to	
	to twitch	to make a sudden, quick movement of a muscle	
	derision [dɪ'rɪʒn]	contempt	
	to despise	to dislike, to regard as worthless	
	thrill	a sudden feeling of excitement	
	to quiver	to tremble, to shudder	
	diaphragm ['daɪəfræm]	*Zwerchfell*	
	smutty	dirty	
	bosom ['bʊzəm]	breasts	
	torrent ['tɒrənt]	a lot of water falling or flowing rapidly	
	to gurgle	to make a bubbling sound	
	to rumble	to make a deep rolling sound	
	vibro-	having to do with vibrations	
	to knead [ni:d]	to press and squeeze *(kneten)*	
	superb [-'-]	excellent	
	specimen	example (of a human being)	
	at the top of one's voice	as loud as possible	
50	**to warble** ['wɔ:bl]	to sing pleasantly with high notes as a bird does	
	Fanny	possibly an allusion to *Fanny Hill*, a pornographic novel by Cleland (1709–1789)	
	cornet	a small trumpet	
	peg	short wooden stick (here: for hanging clothes on)	
	locker	cupboard for one person's clothes, etc.	
	zipper	*Reißverschluß*	*40*
	gesture	bodily movement that demonstrates s. th.	
	undergarment	underclothing	
	stifling	uncomfortable because one can't breathe properly	
	teeming	here: having children, pregnant	
	rabble	noisy and wild crowd	
	evocation [ˌevə'keɪʃən]	here: description of the past	
	nozzle	opening (of a hose, hair-dryer, etc.) *(Düse)*	
	talcum powder ['tælkəm]	perfumed powder for the body	
	scent	perfume	
	eau-de-Cologne [ˌəʊdəkə'ləʊn]	(Fr.) *Kölnisch Wasser*	

	to lay on	to supply, to provide
	to dabble	to splash
	chypre ['ʃɪprə]	a perfume made from sandalwood *(Sandelholz)*
51	**squalid** ['skwɒlɪd]	filthy and untidy
	psychically ['saɪkɪklɪ]	referring to the mind
	midden	a pile of refuse
	friction	here: conflict
	to reek with [ri:k]	to smell, to stink heavily of
	to suffocate ['sʌfəkeɪt]	(fig.) to feel as if you are not getting enough air *(ersticken)*
	intimacy ['ɪntɪməsɪ]	close relationship
	maniacally [mə'naɪəklɪ]	like a crazy person
	to brood over	to worry about and care for
	agonizing	causing mental and physical pain
	to shudder	to tremble
	vibro-vac	i. e. the vibro-vacuum message machine *41*
	out of sorts	unwell
	Dr Wells	possibly an allusion to H. G. Wells (1866–1946), author of science fiction and utopian novels. He was criticized for his views on sexual freedom. (It was Huxley's original intention for his novel to be a satire of H. G. Well's utopian novel *Men Like Gods,* 1923.)
	Pregnancy Substitute	hormones given to make one feel as if pregnant without actually having a child (Note: The modern contraceptive pill – developed in the 50s and 60s – functions as a kind of pregnancy substitute.)
	compulsory [kəm'pʌlsərɪ]	something that has to be done
	brunette	a woman with dark hair
	pelvis	a part of the body between the hips *(Becken)*
	phial ['faɪəl]	a tube-shaped glass bottle
	ovarin	a substance from the ovaries
52	**mammary gland**	the female breast
	placentin	an extract from the placenta
	5cc	5 cubic centimetres
	intravenally	into a vein
	to loathe [ð]	to hate
	(Sigmund) **Freud**	(1856–1939), the founder of psychoanalysis. He believed that most mental problems had to do with sexual drives that were not directed properly usually due to some experience in early childhood, or one's relation to one's parents.
	inscrutable [ɪn'skru:təbl]	difficult to understand, mysterious
	appalling [ə'pɔ:lɪŋ]	dreadful, shocking
	sadism ['seɪdɪzm]	the perverse enjoyment of causing pain (named after the Marquis de Sade, see p. 11/*10*)
	chastity ['tʃæstətɪ]	sexual abstinence, i. e not having any sex

	Samoa [sə'məʊə]	a group of islands in the South Pacific	
	New Guinea ['gɪnɪ]	an island in the West Pacific north of Australia. In the following description Huxley has, no doubt, been influenced by the works of the American sociologist Margaret Mead (1901–1978), whose studies showed that adolescents there had a great deal more sexual freedom than in Western cultures.	
	to tumble	to fall with a rolling movement	
	promiscuous [prə'mɪskjʊəs]	having sexual relationships with a lot of different people	
	hibiscus [hɪ'bɪskəs]	plant with large red or yellow flowers shaped like a bell	
	thatched	(the roof) covered with reeds, straw or other plant material	
	Trobriands [ˌtrəʊ'brɪændz]	a group of coral islands north of New Guinea	
	conception	fertilization of the ovum *(Empfängnis)*	
	ancestral [-'--]	coming from one's past family	
53	**bridge**	usu.: a card game for four players	*42*
	incongruous [ɪn'kɒŋgrʊəs]	strange, out of place	
	monogamy [mə'nɒgəmɪ]	the practice of having only one sexual partner	
	to channel ['tʃænl]	to control and direct s.th. so that it is used for a certain purpose	
	to cite	to quote, to mention as an example	
	emphatically	showing emphasis, very much agreeing	
	axiomatic [ˌæksɪə'mætɪk]	like an axiom, a statement that is accepted as a basic truth without proof	
	utterly	completely	
	indisputable [ˌɪndɪ'spju:təbl]	certain, cannot be denied, there are no arguments against it	
	... I've been having Henry.	i.e. as a sexual partner	
	I like that.	a common ironic phrase with opposite meaning	
	scarlet	bright red	
	defiant [dɪ'faɪənt]	rebellious, refusing to accept criticism	
54	**truculently** ['trʌkjʊləntlɪ]	aggressively, wanting to quarrel	*43*
	jolly well	(coll.) certainly	
	longdrawn	lasting too long	
	jet	here: a thin and forceful stream of water, gas, etc.	
	infectious [-'--]	spreading to others quickly	
	precious ['preʃəs]	here: beloved	
	to spurt	to come out quickly and suddenly in a thin, powerful stream	
	fierce	intensely	
	foamy	*schäumend*	
	urge	here: sexual desire	
	sane	having a healthy mind	

	virtuous ['vɜːtʃʊəs]	good, well-behaved *(tugendhaft)*	
	what with …	because of (all these)	
	temptation	the desire to do s.th. that one knows is wrong *(Versuchung)*	
	remorse [rɪ'mɔːs]	strong feeling of guilt about s.th. one has done; regret	
	in solitude	alone	
55	**stickler (for s.th.)**	a person who insists on a certain kind of behaviour	
	to scrabble	to scrape, to scratch; here: to struggle with, to try to live from	*44*
	crust [krʌst]	surface of the earth, soil	
	to tend	to take care of, to look after	
	axle	part of a vehicle joining two wheels together	
	to bemoan	to express sadness and dissatisfaction about s.th.	
	corpse	dead body	
56	**to coax** ['kəʊks]	to try to gently persuade to do s.th.	
	primal ['praɪml]	most important, basic	
	furtive	hiding so as not to be noticed	
	undergrowth ['---]	bushes, small trees, low plants	
	promiscuity [ˌprɒmɪ'skjuːətɪ]	n. of "promiscuous"	
	arrested	here: that has been stopped	*45*
	current	flow *(Strömung)*	
	appointed channel	chosen course	
	external secretion	i.e. a substitute for mother's milk	
	to lurk [lɜːk]	to wait quietly where one cannot be seen	
57	**consummation** [ˌ--'--]	fulfillment	
	Ford's in his flivver, ... All's well with the world.	cf. the well-known verse, "God's in his heaven, All's right with the world!" from *Pippa Passes* by the English poet Robert Browning (1812–1889)	
	flivver ['flɪvə]	small, cheap, old car	
	pneumatic [njuː'mætɪk]	here: sensuous, sexually pleasing (the word seems to have been first used in this sense by the poet T.S. Eliot (1888–1956) in "Whispers of Immortality": "Grishkin is nice: her Russian eye Is underlined for emphasis; Uncorseted, her friendly bust Gives promise of pneumatic bliss."	
	aisle [aɪl]	central passage	
	to overhear	to hear what s.o. is saying unknown to this person	
	casualness ['kæʒʊəlnes]	behaviour that shows little concern or interest	
	forced	done with great effort, not real	
	savage ['--]	a wild uncivilized person	*46*
	obstacle ['ɒbstəkl]	s.th. that stands in the way	

58	**to encounter**	to be faced with, to have to deal with	
	insurmountable [ˌɪnsəˈmaʊntəbl]	impossible to overcome	
	ancestor [ˈænsestə]	person one is descended from	
	to deliver	here: to rescue	
	to grind one's teeth	i.e. with anger or frustration	
	mutton [ˈmʌtn]	meat of the sheep	
59	**ectogenesis** [ˌektəʊˈdʒenəsɪs]	growth of an embryo outside the mother's body	*47*
	Pfitzner, Kawaguchi	fictitious names; the first possibly suggested by: the German composer Hans Pfitzner (1869–1949)	
	to pet	to stroke or pat s.o. with affection	
	stunted	prevented from growing to the full height	
	indignant	angry	
	round peg … square hole	a person who doesn't fit his or her surroundings	
			48
60	**phosgene** [ˈfɒzdʒiːn] **… hydrocyanic acid**	poisonous gases used in World War I	
	in open order	flying in formation but not close to each other	
	Eighth Arrondissement	(Fr.) a fashionable section of Paris	
	anthrax [ˈænθræks]	highly infectious disease caused by bacillus anthracis	
	anthrax bomb	a bomb consisting of the spores of the bacillus, which are released into the air	
	$CH_3\,C_6\,H_2\,(NO_2)_3$	TNT	
	$Hg\,(CNO)_2$	fulminate of mercury, used as a primer *(Sprengkapsel)* to set off TNT	
	masonry [ˈmeɪsənrɪ]	pieces of stone or bricks from a wall or building	
61	**mucus** [ˈmjuːkəs]	*Schleim*	
	flop	the noise s.th. heavy but soft makes when it falls on s.th.	
	ingenious [ɪnˈdʒiːnɪəs]	especially clever, very inventive	
	Economic Collapse	Huxley no doubt had in mind a more catastrophic version of the Wall Street crash which occurred three years before *Brave New World* was first published.	
	the voices	i.e. the voices from the loudspeakers	*49*
62	**Ending is better than mending.**	cf. the actual proverb, "Mending is better than spending."	
	buttocks	the part of the body one sits on	
	conscription	usu.: officially making people join the army, navy, or air force	
	conscription of consumption	here: making people consume more	
	averted	turned away	
	stitch	act of mending s.th. with needle and thread *(Stich)*	
	… stitches … riches.	cf. the actual proverb, "A stitch in time saves nine." *(Gleich getan ist viel gespart.)*	
	dismal	sad and depressing	

	conscientious objection [ˌkɒnʃɪ'enʃəs]	usu.: refusing to fight in a war for moral reasons; here: refusing to consume more	
	cuff [kʌf]	end of sleeves *(Manschette)*	*50*
	collar ['kɒlə]	part round the neck	
	Simple Lifer	here: a person who wants to live close to nature with few possessions, and refuses to consume more than is necessary	
	to mow down [məʊ]	to slaughter, to kill a large number of people at the same time	
	Golders Green	a suburb to the north of central London	
63	**British Museum**	in London, founded 1753; has one of the world's best collections of antique art and contains the British national library	
	jockey cap	like a cap worn by riders in horse races	
	infinitely ['----]	extremely	
	morocco	a fine soft leather made from goatskin	
	cartridge belt	usu.: a belt for carrying bullets	
	contraceptive [ˌ--'--]	an artificial means of preventing conception	
	Malthusian [mæl'θju:zɪən]	referring to Thomas Robert Malthus, English economist, (1766–1834). In his "Essay on the Principle of Population" he stated his belief that the population of the world would increase at a much faster rate than the increase in agricultural production. He saw war, disease, crime, and famine as necessary for keeping the balance. Malthus's ideas were used at the end of the 19th century to support the movement for family planning and abortion.	
64	**patent** ['peɪtnt]	shiny leather	*51*
	bandolier [ˌbændə'lɪə]	cartridge belt worn across the chest	
	disgrace	s.th. causing shame	
	... introduction ... T-Model	i.e. in 1908	
	fixation of nitrogen ['naɪtrədʒən]	nitrogen *(Stickstoff)* in the air converted into a compound to be used as a fertilizer *(Düngemittel)*	
65	**Community Sing**	organized group singing (explained in full in Chapter V)	*52*
	service	usu.: worship in church *(Gottesdienst)*	
	morphia	= morphium, a drug made from opium; used as a pain-killer	
	cocaine [kəʊ'keɪn]	an addictive narcotic drug made from coca leaves was used in medicine as an anaesthetic	
	to subsidize ['---]	to give official financial help so that s.th. can continue to operate	
	glum	depressed	
66	**to bait**	to torment s.o. by making cruel remarks	
	narcotic [-'--]	causing sleepiness or reducing pain	
	hallucinant [-'---]	causing one to see things that are not real	
	clap	light blow with an open hand, usually in a friendly manner	

	brute	insensitive man, beast	
	soma	in this society: a drug with no side effects. Huxley explains in *Brave New World Revisted* that he took the name from the drug used by an ancient people in India as a part of their religious ceremonies. It did have serious side-effects.	
	to fend off	to refuse to accept	*53*
	proffered	offered	
	gloomy	depressing, sad	
	sentiments	feelings	
	homely	simple, modest	
	hoity-toity	snooty, haughty, arrogant, thinking one is more important than others	
	gonadal ['gɒneɪdəl]	having to do with the sex organs	
	magnesium salt	a salt used to clean out the stomach	
67	**… is better than a damn**	i.e … is better than getting all excited about s.th.	
	physiological [ˌfɪzɪə'lɒdʒɪkl]	having to do with how the body functions	
	stigmata ['stɪgmətə]	signs, marks, characteristics that cause shame	
	peculiarity [pɪˌkju:lɪ'ærətɪ]	strange habit or characteristic	
	to renounce [rɪ'naʊns]	to give up a way of living or a belief	*54*
	to retire	to stop working after a certain age	
	to take to religion	to become religious	
	swine	pig(s)	
	to copulate ['kɒpjʊleɪt]	to have sex	
	leisure ['leʒə]	free time	
	crevice ['krevɪs]	crack, narrow opening	
	crevice of time	i.e. short period of time	
	to yawn [jɔ:n]	to open wide; here: to come up, to appear	
	distraction	an activity that is expected to amuse	
	solid substance of distractions	i.e. the time when they are constantly doing s.th. to keep them busy	
	gorgeous ['gɔ:dʒəs]	lovely	
	East	e.g. India and China, with which Huxley associates exotic ways of life and religions	
	whence	from where	

1. How would you describe the narrative technique used in this chapter? What is its effect?
2. a) "History is bunk" (p. 48/*38*). Discuss the meaning of this Henry Ford quotation, and say why it is quoted by the Controller.
   b) What historical "facts" are added in this chapter? Is there a contradiction involved in the official attitude to history?
3. Henry Ford was a hard-headed businessman, an anti-intellectual and anti-semite. Discuss the significance of Brave New World's confusion of the names Ford and Freud (p. 52/*41*).
4. What system of sexual morality applies in Brave New World?

	salutation	greeting	
	Edzel	probably from Edsel Bryant Ford (1893–1943), Henry Ford's son, who was president of the Ford Motor Company from 1919 to his death	
	parathyroid ['pærə'θaɪrɔɪd]	here: the hormone produced by the parathyroid gland *(Nebenschilddrüse)*	
	Benito	probably from Benito Mussolini (1883–1945), Italian Fascist dictator	
	Hoover	probably from Herbert Hoover (1874–1964), 31st president of the USA (1929–33). It could also be a reference to the vacuum cleaner.	
	recollection	memory	
	to mount	to rise	
	tail	here: corner	
	to gape	to stare in wonder with an open mouth	
	deliciously	here: sweetly, most expressively	
70	**to flush**	to blush, to become red with embarrassment	
	touched	here: *gerührt*	
	to stammer	to stutter, to speak hesitantly	
	choked	not able to breathe properly	*56*
	frank	open, honest	
	unmalicious [ˌʌnmə'lɪʃəs]	with no bad intentions	
	Charing-T	Charing Cross is a district in London. It is also a cross in front of Charing Cross railway station (see p. 39/*31:* "Model-T", "sign of the T".)	
	Hampstead ['hæmpstɪd]	a residential district in North London	
	creaking [-i:-]	squeaking, harsh-sounding	
	simian ['sɪmɪən]	looking like a monkey	
	tunic ['tju:nɪk]	a long jacket that is part of a uniform	
	moron ['--]	very stupid person	
	rapture	extreme feeling of happiness, ecstacy	
	to annihiliate [ə'naɪəleɪt]	to destroy	
	stupor ['stju:pə]	state of being half asleep because of drugs or alcohol	
	doggily expectant	like a dog expecting s. th.	
	adoration	great love and respect (usu. towards God)	
71	**imperious** [ɪm'pɪərɪəs]	with an air of authority	
	to drone	to make a low, monotonous sound	
	well	the vertical space in which the lift goes up and down	
	habitual [-'--]	here: constant	
	to hasten	to rush	
	caress [-'-]	a gentle stroke, a light loving touch	
	rapturously ['----]	full of extreme joy	*57*
	cross	angry	
	hangar ['hæŋə]	a building where airplanes are kept and repaired	
	to retreat	to move away into the distance	

	twinkle	here: brightness
	to unbend	to become straight
	cheery	bright and happy
	chubby	a bit fat and round
	to beam	to smile broadly (*strahlen*)
	manifest ['---]	clear, obvious
	cordiality [ˌkɔːdɪ'ælətɪ]	being warm and friendly
	malice ['mælɪs]	a desire to harm others
72	**temper**	mood
	to afflict	to cause suffering
	I say, ...	expression of surprise (old-fashioned and very upper-class)
	to dive	here: to reach
	plug	thick piece
	to ruminate ['---]	to chew like a cow, or to think about s.th. carefully
	lock-up	garage
	screws	here: rotors
	to shrill	to make a high, sharp sound
	hornet	*Hornisse*
	wasp	*Wespe*
	mosquito	*Stechmücke*
	speedometer [-'---]	an instrument that shows speed
	at the best part	almost
	to diminish [-'--]	to decrease in size, to become less
	mushroom	*Pilz* *58*
	to sprout [spraʊt]	here: to appear to be growing quickly out of the ground
	thin-stalked [stɔːkt]	with a thin stalk *(Stiel)*
	concrete	*Beton*
	vague [veɪg]	here: with a shape that is not clear
	torso	the human body without the head, arms, and legs
	fabulous	unreal, belonging to a fable, or: large and wonderful
	fleshy	fat
	to loll [lɒl]	to lie in a lazy and relaxed manner
73	**octave** ['ɒktɪv]	(mus.) half or double the frequency of a given note
	bumble-bee	*Hummel*
	cockchafer ['kɒktʃeɪfə]	*Maikäfer*
	stag-beetle	*Hirschkäfer*
	to slacken off	to become slower
	horizontal speed	i. e. caused by the forward movement of the helicopter
	stay	*Strebe*
	planes	here: (double) wings, as in early planes
	maggoty ['---]	(appearing to be) full of maggots (*Maden*)
	fore-shortened	appearing to be smaller in the distance
	to gleam	to shine
	Shepherd's Bush	a section of West London

Riemann-surface — Georg Riemann (1826–1866), German mathematician, developed a new kind of geometry that was later used by Albert Einstein. The Riemann surface was a surface with many planes *(Ebene)* to represent complicated mathematical functions.
fives — a game like squash where a ball is hit against the wall with the hand or a stick
court — a small field for a game
Notting Hill — a district in West London
Willesden ['---] — a section of London 6 km to the north-west of the centre
Ealing ['i:lɪŋ] — a suburb of London 10 km to the west
display — public performance
hideous — ugly, disgusting
Hounslow ['haʊnzləʊ] — a section of West London
hectare ['hekteə] — 10,000 square metres (Note that the metric system was not used in Britain in Huxley's day.)
74 **labourer** — worker *59*
Great West Road — actually exists, between London and Feltham
to revitrify [rɪ'vɪtrɪfaɪ] — here: to cover again with a glass-like substance
crucible ['kru:sɪbl] — a pot in which metal or other substances can be melted
to tap — to make a small opening in s. th. to let out the liquid inside
molten — turned into a liquid by very great heat
to dazzle — to shine extremely brightly
incandescence [ˌɪnkæn'desns] — the light caused by heating s. th. to a high temperature
roller — *Walze*
at the tail of — behind
watering-cart — a wagon to spray water
Brentford — a district in West London on the Thames
aphid/pl. **aphides** ['eɪfɪd/'eɪfɪdi:z] — greenfly (*Blattlaus*)
to swarm — to gather together like insects
monorail — riding on, or hanging from one rail
mulberry ['mʌlbrɪ] — dark red berry (*Maulbeere*)
to alight [ə'laɪt] — to land
My word … — exclamation *(Meine Güte)*
Stoke Poges [ˌstəʊk 'pəʊdʒɪz] — small town about 25 km west of central London
downcast ['--] — towards the ground
to light on — to settle on, to fall on
furtively ['fɜ:tɪvlɪ] — done in a quiet and secret way
lest — for fear that
75 **timid** — lacking confidence
to long — (usu.: to long for) to want s. th. very much
to despair of — to give up hope
to humiliate [hju:mɪlɪeɪt] — to make feel ashamed, to hurt s. o.'s pride

	wretched ['retʃɪd]	unhappy	
	to lounge [laʊndʒ]	to stand around doing nothing	*60*
	to staff	to provide with workers	
	offensive	not polite; rude, insulting	
	secure in	sure about	
	dealings	business, relations	
	distressing	upsetting	
	current	at the moment, now	
	physique [fɪ'zi:k]	shape and size of the body and muscles	
	slender in proportion	thin compared to his height	
	inadequacy [ɪn'ædɪkwəsɪ]	being insufficient, not having enough of s. th.	
	self-consciousness	feeling shy and easily embarrassed	
	to haunt [hɔ:nt]	to constantly bother, to plague	
76	**corporeal mass** [kɔ:'pɔ:rɪəl]	the size of a person's body	
	in favour of size	i. e. seeing size as something better	
	proposal	here: a request to a woman to have sex	
	practical joking	tricks that are intended to make s. o. look silly	
	mockery ['--]	ridicule, the act of making fun of the way s. o. behaves	
	to intensify	to increase	
	aroused	brought forth, caused	
	alien ['eɪlɪən]	completely different	
	to slight	to insult	
	to stand on one's dignity	to insist on being treated with respect	
	inferiors	those of lower castes	
	beneficent [bɪ'nefɪsnt]	kind, generous	
	element in which they had their being	i. e. this society in which they existed	
	slackly	slowly and not giving much care	
	reluctance	doing s. th. unwillingly	
	bestial ['bestɪəl]	like a beast	
	rasp	rough harsh sound	
	basement	a floor below the ground floor	
	Fleet Street	a street in central London in which up to recently many newspaper offices were situated	
	The Hourly Radio	probably a parody of *The Times*	
	sheet	(usu. derog.) newspaper	
	gazette [gə'zet]	newspaper	
77	**The Delta Mirror**	probably a parody of the mass circulation *Daily Mirror*	
	padded	with the walls covered with soft material to make them sound-proof	
	Sound-Track	words, music and sound effects	
	Helmholtz	probably from Hermann Ludwig von Helmholtz (1821–1894), German physiologist, physician, physicist, and mathematician. He is known for his investigation of sight and sound.	

	Watson	probably from John Broadus Watson (1878–1958) American psychologist, one of the leading founders of the school of behaviourism, which studied only those kinds of behaviour that could be measured in the laboratory. For this school of thought learning and behaviour could be reduced to stimulus and response.	
	I'll leave you to …	You can …	
	lustrous ['lʌstrəs]	shining	
	briskly	quickly and businesslike	
	springy	*federnd*	
	agile ['ædʒaɪl]	able to move about quickly and easily	
	pillar of his neck	i. e. his neck was like a pillar *(Pfeiler)*	
	his features strongly marked	with a clear-cut face	*62*
	forcible, emphatic	strong, clear, definite	
	lecturer	university or college teacher	
	feely scenario	script for a "feely"	
	knack [næk]	special ability, talent	
78	**verdict** ['--]	opinion, judgement	
	mental excess	i. e. too much intelligence	
	bone and brawn	(coll.) physical size and strength	
	indefatigable [ˌɪndɪ'fætɪgəbl]	never becoming tired	
	committee man	a man who likes to participate in and organize committees	
	mixer	a person who is good at socializing	
	at the bottom	basically, really	
	to waylay [ˌweɪ'leɪ]	to wait for and stop s. o. who is passing to ask s. th.	
	Exmoor ['eksˌmʊə]	a high moorland in southwest England, in northwest Somerset and Devon	
	to cling (clung, clung)	to stay very near, to refuse to go away	
	imploringly	asking, begging earnestly or desperately	*63*
79	**unshaken**	i. e. refusing to change his mind	
	to hold on a course	to stay on the same path even if it is difficult	
	to trail after s. o.	to follow s. o. close behind	
	reproach [rɪ'prəʊtʃ]	an expression of disapproval, words of criticism	
	hypocritical [ˌhɪpə'krɪtɪkl]	saying s. th. one doesn't really believe	
	to be seized with a sudden urge	to suddenly have a desire to do s. th.	
	to cut	to cancel, to no longer continue with s. th.	
	hullabaloo [ˌhʌləbə'lu:]	(coll.) excited comment, uproar	
	shortcoming	fault, defect, failing	
	voluntary ['vɒləntrɪ]	done of s. o.'s free will	
	solitude ['sɒlɪtju:d]	the state of being alone	
	impotence ['ɪmpətəns]	inability to have sex	
	asceticism [ə'setɪsɪzəm]	a simple, strict way of life with no luxuries or physical pleasures	

	to accomplish	to bring to an end	
	pneumatic [nju:ˈmætɪk]	filled with air under pressure (usual meaning)	
80	**intense**	strong, deeply felt	64
	scent organ [sent]	a musical instrument that also produces smells	
81	**to boil down to**	to amount to in the end	
	plaintive	sounding sad and sorrowful	
	uprush ['--]	sudden rise	

1. Note that since the family no longer exists, both surnames and first names have to be given. Discuss why the names of famous 19th and 20th century people should have survived into A.F. 632 – or why Huxley should have chosen them.
2. Describe Brave New World's transport technology. What elements still seem futuristic? What elements now seem dated?
3. What have Bernard, and Helmholtz got in common? What are their main differences?

82

Chapter Five

66

	… Stoke Poges …	see p. 74/*59*. The town is also the burial place of Thomas Gray (1716–1771), who wrote one of the best-known poems in the English language, "Elegy written in a Country Churchyard".	
	tenor ['tenə]	sound, tone	
	external secretion	i.e. milk	
	Trust	here: company that holds property for use in the public interest	
	to low [ləʊ]	to make the typical sound of a cow	
	Farnham Royal ['fɑ:nəm]	a small town 4 km southwest of Stoke Poges	
	incessant	continuing without stopping	
	screech [skri:tʃ]	an unpleasant, high sound	
	metropolis [məˈtrɒpəlɪs]	the large city in an area; here: London	
	to be poised	to be in the air and completely still	
	to fade	to slowly become darker	
	Burnham Beeches	about 5 km north of Farnham Royal	
83	**approach**	path or road to a building	
	pullulation [ˌ--'--]	moving about like a massive group of insects	
	vault [vɔ:lt]	a large curved roof	
	Slough [slaʊ]	an industrial town 30 km west of London	
	crematorium [ˌkreməˈtɔ:rɪəm]	a building where dead bodies are burned (v.: to cremate)	
	to tip	to mark the extreme top of s.th.	67
	smoke-stack	tall chimney	
	phosphorus ['fɒsfərəs]	the chemical element P	
	recovery	here: getting useful substances from waste, recycling	

	telegraphically	briefly, without wasting words	
	treatment	process	
	$P_2 O_5$	phosphorus pentoxide, produced when phosphorus burns	
	perpendicularly [--'----]	vertically *(senkrecht)*	
	All men … equal.	an ironic allusion to the American Declaration of Independence, 1776	
	indispensable [--'---]	absolutely necessary, impossible to do without	
84	**to haunt** [hɔ:nt]	to return again and again, like a ghost	
	wakeful	unable to sleep	
	to soothe [su:ð]	to make calm or quiet	
	to smoothe [smu:ð]	here: to reduce tension	
	stealthy ['stelθɪ]	done in a quiet and secret way	
	conviction	firm opinion or belief	*68*
	bank	here: mass	
	zenith ['zenɪθ]	the area in the sky directly above	
	to descend	to fall	
	chill	unpleasant coldness	
	switchback	railway with sudden upward and downward curves, usually for amusement at a fun-fair	
85	**squirt**	a stream of water or gas forced out of a small opening	
	Westminster	a section of London containing the Houses of Parliament	
	Westminster Abbey	Gothic church where English kings and queens have been crowned since William I, and many famous poets buried.	
	… the outer darkness …	possibly a biblical allusion: "But the children of the kingdom shall be cast out into the outer darkness …" Matthew 8:12	
	… depressing fact …	Huxley is no doubt referring to the belief, widespread among intellectuals of his time, that there is no meaning to be found in the universe to explain human existence; we must face the silence of the universe alone.	
	Calvin	probably from John Calvin (1509–1564), French Protestant reformer who had a great influence on the Puritan religion in England. An ironic allusion: The followers of Calvin have been very restrictive and repressive in their attitude to sex.	
	Stopes	probably from Marie Carmichael Stopes (1880–1958). She was very active in the movement to introduce birth – control.	
	sexophone	word-play on "sex" and "saxophone"	
	colour organ	Attempts to build musical instruments that produced corresponding colours were already made in the 18th century. By the end of the 1920s numerous colour organs and colour pianos had been invented. The noted Austrian composer Arnold Schönberg (1874–1951)	

		composed a piece ("The Lucky Hand") in 1913 which required having colours projected on a screen during the performance.	
	ambergris ['æmbəgri:s]	wax-like substance found in whales and used in perfumes	*69*
	sandalwood ['---]	substance used in perfumes *(Sandelholz)*	
	domed [dəʊmd]	having a large round shape	
	(… ain't no) Bottle	this society's substitute for "mother" (cf. the numerous popular songs about "mother")	
	to five-step	to do a dance in 5/4 rhythm (cf. "two-step", "quickstep", both popular in Huxley's time)	
	to wail [weɪl]	to howl, to moan, to make long and high cries as when in pain	
86	**to moan**	to wail	
	register	(mus.) high or low range of a voice	
	as though the little death were upon them	as if they had just had sex	
	shattering	here: extremely loud	
	ether-music ['i:θə]	synthetic music that sounds as if from the upper atmosphere, from heaven	
	blower	player, musician	
	clean	here: completely	
	A flat major	(mus.) *As-Dur*	
	deturgescence [--'---]	a reduction in swelling	
	diminuendo [-ˌ--'--]	(mus.) decrease in loudness	
	to linger on	to continue longer than expected	
	five-four rhythm	five beats in one bar, an unusual rhythm (unknown in the popular music of Huxley's day, but occasionally used later)	
	to pulse	to beat, to vibrate	
	to charge	to fill	
	expectancy	expecting s. th. to happen soon	
	decanted	this society's version of being born	
	Bottle of mine …	The words of the song seem to be a parody of the "regression" described by Freud – the desire to return to an earlier state of development as a way of avoiding problems, the desire to return to the womb.	
	perennially [pə'renɪəlɪ]	always, constantly	*70*
87	**blues**	musical form often considered the heart of jazz	
	to rock	to move backwards and forwards	
	to veil [veɪl]	to hide	
	genial ['dʒi:nɪəl]	kindly, pleasant	
	to dissolve	to disappear	
	impenetrable [ɪm'penɪtrəbl]	impossible to get through	
	bottled	here: completely in their own world of *soma*	
	to prescribe	to order, to say what must be done	
	drill	frequently repeated exercise	
88	**alternate Thursdays** [-'--]	every other Thursday	

	Aphroditaeum [--'---]	club named after the Greek goddess of love, Aphrodite. Perhaps an allusion to the London gentlemen's club Athenaeum in Pall Mall founded in 1824: Huxley was himself a member.	
	to take leave of	to say good-bye	
	to hail a taxi [heɪl]	to stop a taxi by waving one's hand	
	Carrara [kə'rɑ:rə]	white marble that comes from the northern Italian city of the same name	*71*
	Ludgate Hill	name of street in front of St. Paul's Cathedral (the "Singery"probably stands where the Cathedral once did)	
	to rumble	to make a deep loud sound	
	to catch sight of	to see *(erblicken)*	
	Big Henry	an allusion to Big Ben, which, of course, is part of the Houses of Parliament	
	cab	taxi	
	massed	consisting of a large number of people gathered together	
	having wound himself up	having got ready for an unpleasant task	
89	**inconspicuously** [ˌɪŋkən'spɪkjʊəslɪ]	without attracting attention	
	Obstacle or …	i. e. golf	
	Morgana	perhaps an allusion to fata morgana, an image of s.th. seen upside down in the air, or Morgan le Fay, the wicked witch of Arthurian legend, or the American banker John Morgan (1837–1913). A fourth possibility would be Thomas Hunt Morgan, an American biologist (1866–1945), who won the Nobel prize in 1933 for his work on the influence of chromosomes on heredity.	
	Rothschild ['rɒθtʃaɪld]	name of a powerful family of European Jewish bankers. Lionel Rothschild (1809–1879) became the first Jewish member of the British Parliament.	
	awkward ['ɔ:kwəd]	embarrassing	
	atonement	(usu. theol.) *Sühne, Buße*	
	to scuttle for	to rush to s. th. with short quick steps	
	Bradlaugh ['brædlɔ:]	probably from Charles Bradlaugh (1833–1891) British social reformer. He supported the movement for free speech, birth control, and the right of women to vote.	
	Joanna	possibly an allusion to Joan of Arc (1412–1431)	
	Diesel	allusion to Rudolf Diesel (1858–1913), inventor of the diesel engine	
	Clara	could be named after: – Clara Barton (1821–1912) organizer of the American Red Cross – Clara Ford, wife of Henry Ford – Clara Schumann (1819–1896) composer and pianist, wife of the German composer Robert Schumann	*72*

Deterding — probably from Henri Deterding (1866–1939), from 1901 general manager of the Royal Dutch Shell Company

plump — nicely rounded, a bit fat

lout [laʊt] — rough, impolite person

Engels — probably from Friedrich Engels (1820–1895), German socialist and businessman. After 1850 he lived in England. He was a close intellectual friend of Karl Marx, supporting him financially. Engels helped to write *The Communist Manifesto.*

severely — sternly

Bokanovsky — presumably named after the (fictional) inventor of the "Bokanovski process" (see p. 21/*17*)

Bakunin — probably from Mikhail Bakunin (1814–1876) Russian anarchist revolutionary, who believed in the goodness of man and extreme individualism. He also believed in the violent overthrow of the states existing at his time. With his ideas he came into conflict with Karl Marx.

flaw — weakness, fault

alternation — change from one to the other

90 **to fuse** [fju:z] — to join together totally

choir ['kwaɪə] — here: orchestra

near-wind — something like a wind instrument *(Blasinstrument)*

string — (mus.) stringed instrument, e.g. violin, cello

plangently ['plændʒentlɪ] — having a very expressive and melancholy quality

hymn [hɪm] — usu.: a song praising God, which is sung in church

midriff ['--] — the part of the human body between the waist and chest

to recur — to repeat

to yearn [jɜ:n] — to have a strong desire for s.th. that is difficult to get

bowels ['baʊəlz] — *Gedärm* (here: the innermost emotions)

compassion — sympathy for the suffering of others

… bowels of compassion — an allusion to the First Epistle of John, 3:17: "Whoso hath this world's good, and seeth his brother have need, and shutteth up his bowels of compassion from him, how dwelleth the love of God in him."

to dedicate — to solemnly give a higher purpose to *(weihen)*

tablets … cup … ice cream — The following scene is a parody of the sacrament of the Eucharist (the ritual of the Last Supper); the real service would use bread in the form of wafers, and a chalice of wine.

annihilation [əˌnaɪə'leɪʃn] — total destruction, death

to quaff [kwɒf] — to drink large amounts of s.th.

	stanza	verse *(Strophe)*	
	to clash	to come together in a violent way	
	obsession [-'--]	idea or feeling that takes hold of a person	*73*
	melted bowels	the body, as affected by the music	
91	**benevolence** [bɪ'nevələns]	desire to do good	
	imminence ['ɪmɪnəns]	the fact that something will soon occur	
	... His Coming	a parody of the Christian idea of the Second Coming of Christ, and especially of the Adventists who believed that it was due for the year 1843	
	to initiate [ɪ'nɪʃɪeɪt]	to start	
	exultant [ɪg'zʌltənt]	extremely joyful	
	remote	far away	
	to thrill	to feel sudden strong excitement	
	stretched	here: tense *(gespannt)*	*74*
92	**to quiver**	to tremble, to shake	
	galvanic [gæl'vænɪk]	dramatic, as if produced by an electric shock	
	vibrant ['vaɪbrənt]	full of energy, exciting	
	on a descending scale	(mus.) becoming lower in tone	
	to radiate ['reɪdɪeɪt]	to spread out from a centre	
	solar plexus	*Magengrube*	
	every extremity [ɪk'streməti]	i.e. hands, feet	
	penetrating	affecting the emotions very deeply	
	to expire	to die out, to become silent	
	taut [tɔ:t]	tightly stretched, tense	
	inarticulately [ˌ--'----]	unable to express oneself properly	
	to testify ['---]	to declare in public	
93	**dilirium** [dɪ'lɪrɪəm]	here: wild and excited sound	
	cymbals ['sɪmblz]	plate-shaped percussion instruments *(Becken, Zimbeln)*	
	blown brass	*Blechbläser*	
	fever	here: a state of great exictement and restlessness	
	tom-tomming	Tom-toms are drums associated with the American Indians.	
	to jig	to dance by jumping up and down	*75*
	to stamp	to bring the foot down heavily on the ground	
	to shuffle	to move one's feet along the floor without lifting them	
	preceding [prɪ'si:dɪŋ]	in front	
	in unison ['ju:nɪsn]	(mus.) at the same time and with the same pitch and rhythm	
	slabbily	heavily	
	to resound [rɪ'zaʊnd]	to reflect sound	
	bass [beɪs]	(mus.) a very low male voice	
	to boom	to make a deep resonant sound	
	consummation [--'--]	completion of an act	
	incarnation	a spirit becoming flesh; in Christian theology: God the Son becoming the human being Jesus Christ	

	Orgy-Porgy	obviously a corruption of a well known nursery rhyme, said to be about George IV (King of Great Britain 1820–1830), who led a very promiscuous life: Georgy Porgy, pudding and pie, Kissed the girls and made them cry. When the boys came out to play, Georgy Porgy ran away.
	tattoo [tə'tu:]	continuous beating of the drum as in a military ceremony
	release	here: relief of tension
	liturgical [-'---]	having to do with the fixed form of a church service
	refrain [rɪ'freɪn]	part of a song that is repeated
94	**foetal** ['fi:tl]	of a foetus
	to waver	to become unsteady, to move back and forth
	disintegration	process of breaking up into small pieces
	planetary chairs	i. e. chairs that surrounded the table like planets
	tenderly	lovingly, gently
	to croon	to sing in a soft low voice
	to coo	to say in a soft murmur (like the sound of a dove)
	negro dove [dʌv]	black dove; normally a white dove is used to represent the Holy Spirit
	to hover ['hɒvə]	to remain in the air in one place
	benevolently [-'----]	wishing to be kind and helpful
	prone	lying flat with the face down
	supine ['su:paɪn]	lying on the back face upwards
	... just sung ...	in the real world: Big Ben had just struck ...
	rapture	intense joy 76
	trace	sign or mark of s. th. from before
	agitation	unrest, anxiety, excitement
	vacant ['veɪkənt]	not filled with anything
	satiety [sə'taɪətɪ]	state of being too filled or satisfied
	equilibrium	state of being balanced
	to replenish	to make full again
	unatoned	i.e. not having achieved atonement (cf. p. 89/*71*)
95	**embrace**	having one's arms round s. o. as a sign of love
	pitch	height, level
	agony ['ægənɪ]	great suffering

1. Here is the first verse of Thomas Gray's famous "Elegy Written in a Country Churchyard":
   The curfew[1] tolls the knell[2] of parting day,
   The lowing herd winds slowly over the lea[3]
   The ploughman homeward plods his weary way,
   And leaves the world to darkness and to me.

   1 here: church-bell
   2 here: marks the end
   3 meadow

   Compare with the wording of the first paragraph of this chapter. What is the intended effect?
2. Thomas Gray's poem goes on to refer to the many unknown people buried in the graveyard. How is this part of the poem reflected later in the chapter?

3. Explain Henry's and Lenina's mood in the helicopter.
4. What is being satirized in the Westminster Abbey Cabaret scene? How accurate was it as a prophecy of developments in the field of entertainment?
5. What is the function of a Solidarity Service in Brave New World society? Explain the comic effect of the scene.

96 **Chapter Six** *77*

	odd	strange, peculiar, unusual	
	New Mexico	a state in the southwest of the USA	
	grim	terrible, cheerless, unpleasant	
	no television …	At the time of writing, TV was at the experimental stage both in the USA and in Europe. The first regularly scheduled broadcasts were by the BBC in 1936.	
	laid on	installed (electricity, water, etc.)	
	putrid ['pju:trɪd]	disgusting, awful	
	Jean-Jacques	possibly an (ironic) allusion to Jean Jacques Rousseau (1712–1778), French philospher and author. He rejected the belief that progress in science would automatically increase human happiness.	
	Habibullah	possibly from Habib Ullah, Emir of Afghanistan (1872–1919)	
	prospect	chance of s. th. happening in the future	
	to be entitled to	to have the right to	
	permit	an official written statement giving permission to do s. th.	
	unique [ju:'ni:k]	the only one of this type	
97	**eccentricity** [ˌeksen'trɪsətɪ]	behaviour that is unusual or not socially acceptable	
	rhinoceros [raɪ'nɒsərəs]	*Nashorn*	
	vigorous ['vɪgərəs]	energetic, lively	*78*
	disquieting	causing anxiety, upsetting	
	mania ['meɪnɪə]	an unnaturally strong desire for or interest in s. th.	
	precious little ['preʃəs]	(coll.) very little	
	Torquay [ˌtɔ:'ki:]	town and resort in southwest England	
	Oxford Union	world-famous debating society of Oxford University	
	St. Andrew's	a summer resort in Scotland on the North Sea, famous for its golf courses	
	Lake District	region of lakes and mountains in northwest England, a favourite resort of writers and artists	
	Skiddaw ['skɪdɔ:]	mountain (931 m) in the Lake District	
98	**to mumble**	to speak unclearly	
	semi-demi	half of a half, i. e. quarter	

	to wrestle ['resl]	*ringen*	
	to grumble	to complain	
	obstinately ['----]	refusing to change one's behaviour	
	bout [baʊt]	match, round of a boxing or wrestling match	
	sundae ['sʌndeɪ]	ice cream with a sauce and whipped cream on top	
	jolly	happy, merry	
	A gramme in time saves nine.	another parody of the saying: "A stitch in time saves nine."	*79*
	foam	the white crest of waves	
	to heave	to rise and fall	
	haggard ['hægəd]	tired looking and thin	
99	**distracted**	unable to think clearly because one is troubled by s. th.	
	dashboard	board containing the controls of a car, plane, etc.	
	at random	without any plan or aim	
	to tremolo ['trəmələʊ]	(mus.) to make a slightly shaking effect when singing or playing a violin, etc.	
	falsetto [fɔ:l'setəʊ]	(mus.) a male voice singing unnaturally high	
	hiccough ['hɪkʌp]	*Schluckauf*	
	derisively [dɪ'raɪsɪvlɪ]	mockingly, making fun of s. th. or s. o.	
	blasphemy ['blæsfəmɪ]	saying s. th. very disrespectful of God or holy things	*80*
	distress	anxiety, worry	
	key	(mus.) particular scale of notes, e. g. A flat major; here: tone	
	to enslave	to make into a slave	
100	**to beseech** [bɪ'si:tʃ] (besought)	to ask in a desperate way	
	to preserve intact	to keep whole, not changed, not damaged	
	voluptuous [və'lʌptʃʊəs]	sexually exciting	
	cajolery [kə'dʒəʊlərɪ]	persuading s. o. with praise or pleasant talk	
	to flinch away	to suddenly turn away	
	to prolong	to continue longer than expected	
	at four thousand	i. e. four thousand feet	*81*
101	**to fondle**	to touch gently, to stroke lovingly	
	at a gulp	with one swallow *(auf einen Schluck)*	
	archness	a playful, teasing tone	
	jolt	sudden forceful movement	
	reflectively	thoughtfully	
	inwardly	i. e. in his mind, to himself	
	premature ['premətjʊə]	too soon	
	to stop	here: to block	
102	**audible** ['ɔ:dəbl]	able to be heard	*83*
	spring	usu.: *Sprungfeder*; here: something deep within her mind that could be awakened	
	Never … today	a corruption of the saying: "Never put off till tomorrow what you can do today."	
	to ramble on	to continue to talk in a disorderly way	
	to reel	to become unsteady, or unstable	

	to pronounce	to declare	
	unabashed	not ashamed	
	infant	a child in the first year of life	
	Ford	here, more in the sense of Freud: It was Freud who developed a theory of regression. A person with mental problems might return to an earlier stage of behaviour to protect himself, behaving like an infant, for example.	
	mournful	sad, full of sorrow	
	to evaporate [ɪ'væpəreɪt]	to change into steam and disappear (here fig.)	
	to make your confidences	to tell s. o. about one's personal matters	
103	**to square one's shoulders**	to stand up straight *(die Schultern straffen)*	*83*
	to brace o. s. for s. th.	to prepare o. s. for an unpleasant task	
	to initial [ɪ'nɪʃl]	to sign with the first letters of one's name	
	airily	in a light, cherry manner	
	Fordspeed	cf. "Godspeed", used to wish s. o. success and safety, especially for a journey	
	body	the main text	
	agitated ['ædʒɪteɪtɪd]	troubled, worried	
104	**scrupulously** ['skru:pjʊləslɪ]	very carefully and precisely	
	gross [grəʊs]	rough, impolite, vulgar	
	solecism ['sɒlɪsɪzəm]	s. th. that is not considered to be good manners	
	intrinsically	in itself	
	objectionable	unpleasant, causing disapproval	
	to be betrayed	here: to be tricked into doing s. th.	
	compulsion	a feeling that one has to do s. th.	
	leave	permission to be absent from work, e. g. for a holiday	*84*
	revolting	disgusting, awful	
	oppressive	humid, making you feel very uncomfortable	
105	**to resume** [rɪ'zju:m]	to begin again after stopping	
	gully ['gʌlɪ]	a small narrow valley formed in a hill by heavy rain	
	to persist	to continue to exist	
	consolation	s. th. that gives you comfort when s. th. unpleasant happens to you	
	peal	loud burst of sound	
	to lapse into	to slowly fall into	
	reminiscence [ˌ--'--]	remembering past events	
	on his dignity	expecting his importance (as Director) to be recognized	
	indecorous [ɪn'dekərəs]	showing bad manners or bad taste	*85*
	discreditable	causing shame	
	to vent one's rage	to let out one's anger	
	malignant [-'--]	having or showing the desire to harm s. o.	
106	**inclination**	natural liking or preference	
	indignation	*Entrüstung*	
	righteous ['raɪtʃəs]	feeling of being morally good and just	

	lapse [læps]	failure to continue with a certain standard	
	decorum [dɪˈkɔ:rəm]	proper behaviour	
	transference [ˈ---]	moving a person and his job to another place	
	sub-	smaller and subordinate to the larger unit	
	to swivel	to turn round quickly	
	swagger	walking with a swinging motion to show pride	
	to exult [ɪgˈzʌlt]	to show great pleasure	
	embattled	in a great conflict or battle against s. th.	
	elated	filled with optimism, joyful	
	intoxicating	stimulating, like the effect of alcohol	
	undismayed [ˌ--ˈ-]	without fear or anxiety	
	tonic [ˈtɒnɪk]	good for one's health and strength	
	affliction	suffering or unhappiness	
	whereupon	at which point	
	Bottomless Past	this society's version of the bottomless pit, i. e. hell	
	due	proper, deserved	*86*
107	**of his acquaintance**	i. e. who he knew	
	outburst	sudden expression of emotion	
	deplorable	extremely bad and unpleasant	
	bold	brave, daring	
	presence of mind	ability to stay calm and react quickly in a crisis situation	
	New Orleans [ˈɔ:li:nz]	a city situated on the Mississippi near the Gulf Coast in the state of Louisiana	
	longitude [ˈlɒndʒɪtju:d]	degrees east or west of Greenwich	
	Longitude 95 West	about 25 km east of Houston, Texas	
	Santa Fé	the capital of New Mexico	
	to concede	to admit, to agree to the truth of s. th.	
	aurora bora [ɔ:ˈrɔ:rə]	seemingly named after the aurora borealis, many-coloured lights that can be seen at night near the North Pole	
	caffeine solution [ˈkæfi:n]	something like coffee	
	plant	here: machinery, equipment	
108	**racquet** [rækɪt]	a game similiar to tennis	
	wearily	very tiredly	*87*
	warden [ˈwɔ:dn]	a person who looks after a place, a building, etc.	
	brachycephalic [ˌbrækɪsɪˈfælɪk]	having a short almost round head	
	adapted to	fit, suitable for	
	was a mine of …	was a rich source of …	
109	**Grand Canyon** [ˈkænjən]	deep, steep valley formed by the Colorado River in northwest Arizona; one of the natural wonders of the world	
	mind's eye	imagination	
	meter	a device that measures s. th. (here: how much has been used)	
	indefatigably [ˌɪndɪˈfætɪgəblɪ]	without getting tired	
	cue [kju:]	any word or phrase that serves as a signal to do or say s. th.	

	serenely	peacefully, calmly	
	rapt	showing extreme interest	
	suggestive	putting certain ideas or associations into one's mind	*88*
	to nibble	to take tiny bites of s. th.	
	to countersign	to sign a document that has been signed by another person	
	to leer	to grin suggesting sexual interest	
110	**simulated**	pretended, not real	
	are destined to …	it is their fate, what must happen	
	decilitre ['desɪli:tə]	1/10 of a litre	
	to tap	to strike lightly	
	inexorably [-'----]	not stopping because it cannot be changed	
	half-breed	a person with parents of two different races	
	repulsive	disgusting, revolting	
	monstrous	shocking	
	superstition	irrational beliefs, e.g. in magic *(Aberglaube)*	
	totemism ['təʊtəmɪzəm]	the belief among American Indians that a group has a spiritual connection to a plant or animal, and this totem, i.e. plant or animal, can protect the group	
	ancestor worship	a belief that the dead exist as spirits and have the power to control the living	
	extinct	here: no longer spoken in the "civilized" world	
	Zuñi ['zu:njɪ]	language spoken by a group of American Indians living in western New Mexico	
	Athapascan [ˌæθə'pæskən]	a group of American Indian languages including the languages of Alaska and northwest Canada, the coast of Oregon and California, and the Navajo and Apache languages of the southwestern United States.	
	porcupine ['pɔ:kjʊpaɪn]	*Stachelschwein*	
	ferocious [fə'rəʊʃəs]	fierce, wild	
	venomous ['venəməs]	poisonous	
	lizard ['lɪzəd]	*Eidechse*	
	to dash	to rush	*89*
	incompetence	lack of ability or skill	
111	**dejected**	depressed, sad	
	to be subjected to s. th.	to have to go through an experience, to undergo	
	resources [rɪ'sɔ:sɪs]	here: strength	
	trial	crisis one has to go through, difficult task	
	stoically ['stəʊɪkəlɪ]	without complaining, accepting the circumstances, from an ancient Greek philosophy stoicism, which believed you should accept your destiny	
	to be appalled [ə'pɔ:ld]	to be shocked	
	stoicism ['stəʊɪsɪzm]	willingness to accept one's destiny, to put up with suffering (from the ancient Greek Stoics, a school of philosophy)	

112	**was and will**	i. e. the past and the future
	roots and fruits	i. e. the past and the future
	octoroon [ˌɒktəˈruːn]	a white person with 1/8 negro blood
	to recite	to list from memory
	pueblo [ˈpwebləʊ]	a village inhabited by an Indian tribe such as the Hopi or Zuñi in the southwestern United States
	Malpais [ˌmælpaˈiːs]	Spanish for "bad land". It lies between the Navajo and Acoma Indian Reservations in the northwest part of New Mexico.
	crag [kræg]	high steep rough rock
	peak	top of a mountain
	table-topped	large and flat, with steep sides
	mesa [ˈmeɪsə]	(Span.) a flat-topped kind of mountain common in the southwestern United States
	irresistibly	too strong to be stopped
	mosaic [məʊˈzeɪɪk]	a number of things seen together that seem to have a design
	unrotted	not yet decomposed *(unverwest)*
	carcass [ˈkɑːkəs]	body of a dead animal
	tawny [ˈtɔːnɪ]	brownish yellow colour
	steer	a castrated ox raised for beef
	coyote [kɔɪˈəʊtɪ]	a small wolf that lives in the western USA
	turkey buzzard [ˈbʌzəd]	a large dark bird with a bare red head and neck that eats dead animals *(Cathartes aura)*
	to fulminate	to explode with noise and violence
	poetic justice	when s. th. bad happens to s. o. who really deserves it
	to score	to achieve, to be successful in getting
	to electrocute [ɪˈlektrəkjuːt]	to kill with an electric current
113	**to drop off to sleep**	to fall asleep
	Taos … Ojo Caliente	Huxley has taken some liberties with geography: these places could only be overflown by taking a zig-zag route. (At the time of writing, Huxley had not yet visited New Mexico. All his information, especially that on Indian customs, he got from books, or from his friend, the writer D.H. Lawrence, who had lived there for a while.)
	Taos [taʊs]	an Indian pueblo in New Mexico, 60 km north of Santa Fé. The nearby town of Taos is a well known resort and art colony.
	Tesuque [teɪˈsʊːkeɪ]	a pueblo 16 km north of Santa Fé
	Nambé [næmˈbeɪ]	a pueblo 30 km north of Santa Fé
	Picuris [ˌpiːkʊˈriːs]	a pueblo 30 km south of Taos 2,300 metres high
	Pojoaque	a pueblo between Nambé and Tesuque, now a ruin
	Sia	a pueblo of the eastern Keresan Indians, 60 km west of Santa Fé
	Cochiti [ˈkəʊtʃɪtɪ]	a pueblo of the eastern Keresan Indians, 40 km northeast of Sia. It is famous for the drums that are used in ceremonies.

Laguna [-'--]	a village of the western Keresan Indians, 60 km west of Albuquerque in central New Mexico
Acoma	a pueblo on a steep-sided mesa 109 m high at an altitude of 2,100 m, known as the "sky city", to the west of Laguna. It has been inhabited by Indians since the 12th century.
Enchanted Mesa	flat-top sandstone mountain 131 m high near the publo of Acoma. There are many Indian legends associated with it.
Zuñi	pueblo in western New Mexico near the Arizona border
Cibola ['si:bəʊlə]	forested area east of the Zuñi Indian Reservation and west of the Malpais
Ojo Caliente	an Indian settlement within the Zuñi Indian Reservation about 20 km southwest of Zuñi *91*
sullen ['sʌlən]	showing a bad temper, gloomy
tame	not fierce, not wild (usually said of animals)

1. What are the main differences (of opinion, of attitude, etc.) between Bernard and Lenina?
2. In what way are they affected by each other's views?
3. What solecism did the DHC commit (p. 103/*83*)? And why did he commit it?
4. Consider the scenes of arrival at the hotel and the Reservation as a parody of American society.
5. Explain the symbolic significance of the electric fence.
6. What crisis does Bernard face? Explain his changing feelings about it.

114

Chapter Seven

92

becalmed	unable to move because there is no wind
strait [streɪt]	a narrow passage of water between two land masses, e.g. the Straits of Gibraltar
channel	i.e. the valley on each side of the mesa
precipitous [-'---]	extremely steep
to slant	to extend from a high to a low level
prow [praʊ]	raised front part of a ship
outcrop	a rock that can be seen above the surface
block above block …	Many Indian pueblos have buildings (of clay or stone) up to five stories high.
stepped	forming steps
straggle	a group without any order
criss-cross	things continually crossing each other
precipice ['presɪpɪs]	a very steep cliff
sheer	almost vertically
to reciprocate [-'---]	to return s.th. felt
to quicken one's pace	to walk faster
115 **gunwale** ['gʌnl]	upper edge of a ship, i. e. the top of the mesa
impending	hanging in a threatening way
projection	a piece of rock sticking out
ravine [rə'vi:n]	deep narrow steep-sided valley

	companion ladder	(on a ship) a ladder from the deck to a cabin	*93*
	all but inaudible	nearly impossible to hear	
	at others	at other times	
	eagle	a large, strong bird of prey often used as a symbol of power, of immortality, or the soul. It played an important role in the rituals of the Pueblo Indians.	
	crevice [ˈkrevɪs]	narrow opening in a rock	
	oppressively	unpleasantly	
	resemblance	similiarity in appearance	
	padding	soft sound made by footsteps	
	daubing [ˈdɔ:bɪŋ]	spot of paint carelessly smeared on s. th.	
	ochre [ˈəʊkə]	brownish-yellow	
	braided with	woven together with	
	flannel [ˈflænl]	soft light woollen cloth	
	diadem [ˈdaɪədem]	crown	
	gaudily	with colours that are a bit too bright	
	bracelet [ˈbreɪslət]	band worn round the wrist or arm	
	necklace [ˈnekləs]	band worn round the neck	
	turquoise [ˈtɜ:kwɔɪz]	a greenish-blue semi-precious stone, used a lot in Indian jewelry	
	bead	a small, round piece of glass, wood or stone *(Perle)*	
	moccasin [ˈmɒkəsɪn]	soft shoe made of animal skin worn by Indians	
116	**to writhe** [raɪð]	to twist or roll about	
	… they were snakes.	Huxley is describing the Snake Dance of the Hopi Indians. Snakes were thought to be bringers of fertility to man and his crops. In midsummer the snakes were thought to be bringers of rain. A special group of Indians would go out in four directions to find snakes, dance with them, and then carry them out in four directions to bring rain.	
	limp	not stiff, hanging loosely	
	indignant	feeling or showing anger	
	… cleaniness … fordliness …	This society's version of the saying "Cleaniness is next to godliness," originated by John Wesley (1703–1793), founder of Methodism	*94*
	sterilization	killing of all bacteria, all (undesired) forms of life	
	rung	the part of the ladder one steps on	
	wrinkled	with the lined skin that comes with age	
	obsidian [ɒbˈsɪdɪən]	a dark glass-like rock	
117	**bristle**	short stiff hair	
	wisp	small, thin, untidy bunch of s. th.	
	emaciated [ɪˈmeɪʃɪeɪtɪd]	extremely thin and weak	
	fleshless	without any muscle or fat	
	unmoved	not affected by feelings	
	ratio [ˈreɪʃɪəʊ]	proportion of one thing to another	
	transfusion	putting the blood of one person into another	
	metabolism [məˈtæbəlɪzm]	*Stoffwechsel*	

	unimpaired	not weakened or damaged	
	orbit	here: the space in which the eyes can move *(Augenhöhle)*	
	to hobble	to walk with difficulty because there's something wrong with the feet or legs	*95*
	unprecedented	never having happpened before	
118	**oversight** ['əʊvəsaɪt]	mistake	
	thick and fast	in great numbers and quickly	
	indecent	improper, obscene	
	to go out of one's way to do s. th.	to make a great effort to do s. th.	
	outrageous	shocking, very offensive	
	to generate	to produce, to cause to exist	
	ophthalmia [ɒf'θælmɪə]	an infection of the eye (Huxley himself had a serious eye infection while at Eton.)	
	to distract	to draw a person's attention away from s. th.	
	goitre ['gɔɪtə]	a swelling of the thyroid gland *(Kropf)*	
	lice	pl. of "louse": an insect parasite	
	to dart	to move suddenly and quickly	
	mutely	silently	
	access ['ækses]	means of entering s. th.	
	grease	fat that has been used for cooking	
119	**shaft**	ray, beam	
	threshold	line in a doorway which divides in from out *(Schwelle)*	*96*
	masonry ['meɪsənrɪ]	s. th. built with stones or bricks	
	clay	a material found in the earth and used for making bricks, pottery, etc. *(Ton)*	
	chamber	room (Huxley is describing the "kiva" which the Pueblo Indians use for secret religious ceremonies. It represents the entrance to the lower world and the place from which life came to this world. It is entered into through a hole in the roof, from which a ladder leads to the floor.)	
	hatchway	the hole in the roof of the kiva	
	subterranean [ˌsʌbtə'reɪnɪən]	underground	
	flute-playing	The flute ceremony was a part of the Hopi fertility dance.	
	remorseless	here: never ending	
	persistence	continuing to do s. th. in spite of opposition	
	to neigh [neɪ]	to make the high sound of a horse	
	treble	high voice	
	… women's answer.	Women played an important role in the social and religious life of the Pueblo Indians, much more than the warlike tribes to the north of New Mexico. For the Zuñi and Hopi the female line of descent was considered more important, and married couples usually lived with the wife's family. Houses and gardens were owned by women But: the religious rites in the kiva were (and are) for men only.	

	affirmation	solemn declaration	
120	**innocuous** [ɪ'nɒkjʊəs]	harmless	
	ghastly ['gɑ:stlɪ]	horrible	
	troop	large group	
	semblance	resemblance, likeness	
	… masked …	Huxley is describing men wearing masks to represent “kachinas” or invisible life spirits that emerge from the underground. The Pueblo Indians had a great deal of respect for these spirits, because they were thought to control the rain needed for the spring crop.	
	chest	wooden box *(Truhe)*	*97*
	mottled ['mɒtld]	with irregular markings	
	undulating ['ʌndjʊləɪtɪŋ]	moving gently up and down	
	corn meal	Corn meal *(Maismehl)* and water were sprinkled on the snakes to ensure a successful harvest. (Corn was the main crop for the Pueblo Indians, which made it possible to live in village communities and not have to be constantly on the move to hunt for food.)	
121	**painted … eagle**	Among the Pueblo Indians, captive eagles were killed for their feathers and buried in a special place. The feathers were thought to have magical qualities, as “the carrier of the wind”, i.e. the breath of life (EJL). It was also believed that the dead eagle could take messages to the spirits.	
	man … nailed to a cross …	It seems that some elements of the Christian religion have been accepted by these (fictional) Indians. During the 16th and 17th centuries when the Spanish invaded and conquered the Southwest and Mexico many attempts were made to convert the Indians.	
	self-sustained	not supported by anything	
	breech-cloth [bri:tʃ]	*Lendentuch*	
	plaited ['plætɪd]	braided, woven together	
	… raised his whip	Puberty rites involving beating with a wooden stick have been observed among the Hopi Indians. But the extreme violence of the initiation ceremony described in the following passage is *not* typical of the Pueblo Indians. It is, however, possible that the practice of whipping one another/oneself could have been learnt from the Spanish missionaries (many of whom whipped themselves as a penance).	
	the whistle of the lash	the sound of the whip moving through the air	
	the coyote [kɔɪ'əʊtɪ]	i.e. the coyote–man, representing a kachina	
	to stagger	to walk unsteadily	*98*
	to pitch	to fall suddenly	

	thrice	three times (an important number in religion and myths)	
:2	**nether world** ['neðə]	lower world, underground i.e. the kiva	
	straw-coloured	yellow, like the stems of ripe wheat *(Stroh)*	
	bronzed [brɒnzd]	brown from the sun	
	morrow	used at the time of Shakespeare for "morning"	
	... most unhappy gentleman ...	a line which sounds Shakespearean, though not from any particular play	
	bloodstain	spot of blood	
	... damned spot?	partly a quotation frrom Shakespeare's *Macbeth,* V, i (where Lady Macbeth expresses her feeling of guilt while sleepwalking)	
123	**Palowhtiwa**	also spelt Pahlowahtiwa, name of a Zuñi chief	*99*
	The multitudinous seas incarnadine.	a quotation from *Macbeth,* II, ii (what Macbeth says shortly after he kills Duncan); incarnadine = red	
	lavish	here: dramatic, flamboyant	
	... for my complexion	= for the colour of my face. An allusion to Shakespeare's *The Merchant of Venice,* II, i, where the dark-skinned Prince of Morocco says to Portia, "Mislike me not for my complexion, ..."	
	deprivation [ˌdeprɪ'veɪʃn]	lack or loss of s. th.	
	Pookong	an Indian God probably invented by Huxley. The name bears a resemblance to the war-God Püükon, and also to the Great Serpent of the Hopis, Palülukong, a being who "comes from the South to bring fertility to crops and man". But the young man is obviously talking about the painted eagle of page 121/*97*.	
	defiant [dɪ'faɪənt]	bold, openly resisting	
	... dogskin	light brown	
	auburn ['ɔ:bən]	reddish brown	
	novelty ['nɒvltɪ]	s. th. completely new and different	
	overcome [ˌ-'-]	affected deeply, full of emotion	
	diversion [daɪ'vɜ:ʃn]	something that turns one's attention away from s. th. else	
124	**Other Place**	i. e. Brave New World	
	to prick up one's ears	to listen carefully	
	Tomakin	The suffix *-kin* is like the German *-chen* or *-lein.*	*100*
	squalor ['skwɒlə]	the condition of being very dirty because of poverty	
	famine-stricken	showing the effect of not having enough to eat	
	garbage	rubbish	
	hoarse [hɔ:s]	rough-sounding	
	stout [staʊt]	fat and heavy	
	squaw	Indian woman	
125	**to shudder**	to shake because of fear, cold, or shock	
	flabbiness	looseness of the skin	
	to sag	to hang loosely	

	blotch	large irregular mark (on the skin, etc.)	
	bloodshot	with the blood-vessels visible (in the white part of the eye)	
	ragged ['--]	old and torn	
	torrent	flood, violently flowing stream (here fig.)	
	bulge	i. e. the stomach	
	slobberingly	*sabbernd*	
	blubbered	here: red and full of tears from crying	*101*
	to finger	to touch with the fingers	
	adorable	charming, lovely	
	velveteen [ˌvelvɪ'tiːn]	a cheap cotton (or viscose) material made to look like velvet	
	mescal	an alcoholic drink made from the maguey plant, which grows in the southwestern United States and Mexico	
126	**Popé**	The name is that of a medicine man of the Pueblo Indians who successfully revolted against the Spanish oppressors in 1680. Until his death in 1690, he tried to wipe out all traces of the Christian religion and Spanish culture.	
	peyotl [peɪ'əʊtl]	a drug that produces visions and changes in the perception of time, sense, and mood. It comes from a cactus and is used in the rituals of some of the native religions. Huxley, himself, experimented with such drugs later in life.	
	Chelsea ['tʃelsɪ]	a residential district of southwest London	
	ecstatically	with great joy	
	to contemplate	to think deeply and thoughfully about s. th.	
	to ooze [uːz]	to flow slowly	
	involuntary [ɪn'vɒləntrɪ]	done without intention	
	aseptic [ˌeɪ'septɪk]	free from bacteria	*102*
	Streptocock ... W.C.	*BNW*'s version of the nursery rhyme: Ride a cock-horse to Banbury Cross To see an old lady upon a white horse. Rings on her fingers, and bells on her toes, She shall have music wherever she goes.	
	streptocock	streptococcus, a bacterium that causes a sore throat	
	gee [dʒiː]	what is said to a horse to get it to move faster	
	Banbury ['bænbərɪ]	town in Oxfordshire in central England. The cross in the nursery rhyme was destroyed by the Puritans in 1602, and replaced with a new one in 1859.	
127	**lunatic** ['---]	crazy person	
	confidentially	in a way that others should not hear what you are saying	
	to shrink	here: to suddenly move back from s.th. because of fear	
	embryopoison	i.e. alcohol	
	to tug	to pull hard	

	untainted [ʌnˈteɪntɪd]	pure, unspoiled (here: without the reek from woman's mouth)	
128	**Waihusiwa**	invented name	*103*

1. Explain the significance of the eagle. Make a report about how the eagle is used in the ceremonies of the Hopi and Zuñi Indians and/or the use of the eagle in European literature and mythology.
2. Compare Lenina's and Bernard's reactions to the pueblo and the Indians living there.
3. What is the purpose of the Indian ceremony?
4. Describe the visitors' first impressions of John the Savage.
5. What can Bernard deduce about the DHC, Linda and John?
6. How has Linda been able to cope with Indian civilization and bringing up John?

129 ## Chapter Eight *104*

	inconceivable [ˌɪŋkənˈsiːvəbl]	difficult to imagine	
	tortilla [tɔːˈtiːjə]	(Span.) round thin cake made of cornmeal, especially eaten in the southwestern USA and Mexico	
	Bye, Baby Banting …	*BNW's* version of the nursery rhyme: Bye, baby bunting, Father's gone a-hunting, Mother's gone a-milking, Sister's gone a-silking, And brother's gone to buy a skin To wrap the baby bunting in.	
	Banting	possibly an allusion to Sir Frederick Grant Banting (1891–1941), who discovered insulin with J.J. Macleod in 1921 at the University of Toronto, Canada. Banting shared the 1923 Nobel Prize for Medicine with Macleod.	
130	**to wriggle** [ˈrɪgl]	to twist from side to side with short quick movements	*105*
	latch [lætʃ]	bar which can be raised and lowered to open/close a door	
	wooden things …	i.e. a loom *(Webstuhl)*	
131	**gourd** [gʊəd]	a fruit whose shell is hollowed out for use as a bottle	
	upset	here: knocked over	*106*
	mule [mjuːl]	an animal that is half donkey and half horse	
	fringe	edge consisting of loose threads	
132	**to wrench s. th. free** [rentʃ]	to get s. th. out by pulling hard with a violent twisting movement	
133	**Inspector**	Warden of the Reservation	*107*
	… little animals in his hair …	i.e. lice *(Läuse)*	
134	**by the hour**	for many hours	*108*

	Transformer … Wet and Dry	elements of the mythology of the Zuñi Indians about the creation of the world	
	Awonawilona	name based on a Zuñi phrase meaning "the one who guides our road," i. e. "the one who directs our life" (EJL)	
	Earth Mother	presumably from the Zuñi idea *awitalensita,* "the land from which man grew" (EJL)	
	Sky Father	fictional, not in the Zuñi tradition (which does, however, have a "Sun Father") (EJL)	
	Ahaiyuta, Marsailema	In the Zuñi tradition, *Ahaiyuta* is the generic name for the twin war gods; *Marsailema* is the given name for the elder of the two. (EJL)	
	Etsanatlehi	fictional goddess, not in the Zuñi tradition (EJL)	
	Black Stone at Laguna	a western Keresan concept, not in the Zuñi tradition (EJL)	
	Our Lady of Acoma	the Virgin Mary as worshiped by the Indians of Acoma	
135	**charcoal** ['tʃɑ:kəʊl]	coal made from wood (sticks of it can be used for drawing)	
	THE CAT IS ON THE MAT	one of the more common sentences which (up to the early 1950s) were used to teach children to read	
	THE TOT …	*BNW* version of such sentences	
	tot	young child	
	… in the pot	i. e. in the bottle, or test tube (instead of the original phrase, "… *on* the pot")	
136	**backward**	less developed	*109*
	calcium carbonate	$CaCO_3$	
	Fog of Increase	in Zuñi mythology: created by Awonawilona in the process of forming life	
	womb [wu:m]	*Schoß*	*110*
	binding ['baɪndɪŋ]	covering of a book that holds the pages together	
	to sip	to drink slowly	
137	**Antelope**	see page 110/*88* under "totemism"	
	Kiva	see page 119/*96* under "chamber"	
	Nay, but to live … sty	Shakespeare's *Hamlet,* III, iv (what Hamlet says to his mother, who has married his uncle, the murderer of his father)	
	nay [neɪ]	(arch.) no	
	rank	smelling badly	
	enseamed [ɪn'si:md]	greasy	
	to stew [stju:]	to cook slowly in water or juice	
	to honey	to say sweet things	
	sty [staɪ]	place where pigs are kept (here fig.)	
	Corn Song	part of the Corn Dance, a fertility ceremony (see p. 120/*97*)	
	carved	cut in decorative patterns (here, with some ritual significance)	
	kiathla … tsithl	invented language	
	A man can smile … villain.	*Hamlet,* I, v (what Hamlet says after his father's spirit tells him that Hamlet's uncle murdered his father): "… one may smile, and smile, and be a villain"	

	villain ['vɪlən]	wicked or evil person	
	Remorseless … villain.	*Hamlet,* II, ii (what Hamlet says about his uncle)	
	remorseless [rɪ'mɔ:sles]	without pity	
	treacherous ['tretʃərəs]	likely to betray trust, deceitful	
	lecherous ['letʃərəs]	always interested in sexual pleasure	
	kindless	(arch.) unnatural	
138	**to not be able to make head or tail of s. th.**	to not be able to understand s. th.	*111*
	to strangle	to kill by pressing on the throat	
	giddy ['gɪdɪ]	dizzy, feeling unsteady	
	When … bed …	*Hamlet,* III, iii (when Hamlet decides not to kill his uncle while his uncle is praying)	
	incestuous	having to do with sexual relations with a close relation	
	to stab	to push a knife into s. o.	
139	**to work**	here: to form with one's hands	*112*
	shallow	not deep	
	to hoop	here: to form into a hoop *(Ring, Reifen)*	
	rim	upper edge	
140	**crooked** ['krʊkɪd]	deformed, twisted, not in the proper shape	
	parody ['pærədɪ]	s. th. so badly done it seems to be a mockery	
	to moisten	to make wet	
	to fashion	to give a certain form to s. th.	
	A, B, C, Vitamin D …	There are many ABC nursery rhymes. This one is obviously a *BNW* one learned from Linda.	
	cod [kɒd]	*Kabeljau*	
	absorbing	completely taking up one's attention	
	to clench	to close tightly	*113*
	pinch	the amount that can be held between the fingers *(Prise)*	
	pinch of corn meal	here: a symbol of fertility	
141	**to bear, bore, borne**	here: to carry in one's mind, or to other places	
	rank	line or row	*114*
	to dodge	to move quickly and suddenly to one side to avoid getting caught	
	to hover [hɒvə]	here: to stand around waiting for s. th.	
	on the fringes	at the edge	
	to bleach	to cause to become white because of chemicals or sunlight	
	bruise [bru:z]	a dark mark on the skin caused by an injury	
142	**Tomorrow and tomorrow …**	Shakespeare's *Macbeth,* V, v (after Macbeth learns of his wife's death and realizes that his situation is rather desperate)	
	plaintive ['pleɪntɪv]	expressing sadness	
	gush	a sudden outflow of s. th.	
	confidingness	from "to confide in s. o.", i. e. to tell s. o. one's secret thoughts	

	… into those mountains …	This idea of testing oneself before God can be found in the Bible, e.g. Exodus in the Old Testament where Israel is tested in the wilderness; also Matthew 4:1–12 and Luke 4:2.	*115*
143	**to crucify**	to execute s.o. by tying to a cross	
	puckered ['pʌkəd]	*runzelig*	
	temple	*Schläfe*	
	pitiful	causing you to feel pity	
	squeamish ['skwi:mɪʃ]	easily sickened by the sight of blood, etc.	
	deformity	an imperfection of the body that can be seen	
	to elaborate	to work out in detail, to plan	
144	**asset** ['æset]	s.th. of value	*116*
	to make up for s.th.	to compensate for s.th.	
	excess	too much of s.th.	
	Miranda	main character in Shakespeare's *The Tempest*	
	O Wonder! …	*The Tempest V, i* (see p. 3/3); the full quotation is: "O, wonder! How many goodly creatures are there here! How beauteous mankind is! O brave new world That hath such people in't!"	
	lustrous	shining	
	to falter	to weaken, to become unsteady	
	perplexed	puzzled, confused	

1. In what way is John's "story within a story" different in style and tone from the rest of the novel?
2. Explain Linda's ambivalent attitude towards her son John – and John's confused feelings for his mother.
3. Why does Shakespeare have such an attraction for John? (And is it plausible that he would understand Shakespeare?)
4. For what reasons does Bernard want John to go back to civilization with him? And for what reasons is John happy to go?

145

Chapter Nine

117

	to embark for	(fig.) to go on a ship, i.e. to start on a trip	
	lunar	having to do with the moon	
	in time	i.e. in the real world again	
	pensive	thinking deeply about s.th.	
	insomnia	inability to sleep at night	
	fruitless	without results	
	agave [ə'geɪvɪ]	a tropical flower found in the southwest United States and Mexico	
	safe as helicopters	*BNW* version of the saying, "safe as houses"	
	Whitehall	site of the main government offices near the Houses of Parliament in London	
146	**boom**	here: deep loud voice	*118*
	deferential [ˌdefə'renʃl]	showing great respect for a person in a higher position	

147	**an electrolytic shave** [ˌ---ˈlɪt-]	shaving by burning off hairs with an electric current	
	televisor	television set	
	a leisured luncheon [ˈleʒəd]	lunch taken in an unhurried and relaxed way	
	essential being	soul, personality	*119*
	faint	about to lose consciousness, weak	
	spare	extra	
	delight	joy, great pleasure	
	zip	here: the sound of opening or closing a zipper	
	enchanted	delighted, charmed	
	zippi-camiknicks [ˈzɪpɪ ˈkæmɪˌnɪks]	an invented word similiar to camiknickers *(Hemdhöschen)*	
	floury [ˈflaʊrɪ]	as if covered by flour *(Mehl)*	
148	**nostrils** [ˈnɒstrəlz]	the openings at the end of the nose	
	musky [ˈmʌskɪ]	smelling of musk *(Moschus)*	
	He crammed his thieveries …	cf. Shakespeare's *Troilus and Cressida,* IV, iv, where Troilus says to Cressida: "Injurious Time now with a robber's haste Crams his rich thiev'ry up, he knows not how."	
	to cram [kræm]	to stuff	
	thievery	stolen goods	
	landing	a level space between two sets of stairs	
	ajar [əˈdʒɑː]	slightly open	
	to peer [piːə]	to look closely and carefully	
	zippyjamas	invented word: pyjamas with zippers	
	melted	here: completely relaxed in deep sleep	
	infinity	endlessly large number	
	short of	less than	
	appointed	fixed, decided on in advance	
	to clasp [klɑːsp]	to hold tightly	
	Her eyes … harsh …	*Troilus and Cressida,* I, i (where Troilus reacts to what Pandarus has been saying about Cressida)	
	gait [geɪt]	way of walking	
	handlest in thy discourse	(arch.) You speak of … in your conversation	
	reproach	shame, disgrace	*120*
	seizure	(here arch.) touch	
	cygnet [ˈsɪgnɪt]	young swan	
	down	soft fine feathers	
	On the white wonder … sin.	Shakespeare's *Romeo and Juliet,* III, iii; slightly changed from the original, where Romeo says, speaking of flies: "They may seize On the white wonder of dear Juliet's hand, And steal …"	
	immortal	never dying	
	vestal modesty [ˈmɒdɪstɪ]	pure, untouched virtuousness	
149	**on the verge of contact** [vɜːdʒ]	very near to touching	
	profane	to treat (s.th. holy) in a disrespectful way	

	Dare to profane …	cf. *Romeo and Juliet,* I, v where Romeo says to Juliet: “If I profane with my unworthiest hand This holy shrine, the gentle sin is this: My lips, two blushing pilgrims, ready stand To smooth that rough touch with a tender kiss.”
	to reflect	to think
	detestable	worthy of being hated
	localized itself	made clear where it was
	to scramble to one’s feet	to stand up hastily as when in a panic
	to vault [vɔ:lt]	to jump (over s. th.)

1. How does Bernard manage to get a permit from Mustapha Mond?
2. What inner conflict does John have upon discovering Lenina fast asleep? What makes the scene hilarious?

150

Chapter Ten

121

	Bloomsbury ['blu:mzbərɪ]	a district of central London that contains the British Museum, part of the University of London, and many publishers’ offices. In the 1920s many artists, intellectuals and writers known to Huxley lived there.
	hive	a structure in which bees live and store honey; here: a place with a lot of busy people
	to lash [læʃ]	to wave sharply to and fro like a whip
	to burrow ['bʌrəʊ]	to move into s. th. by digging
	gorged [gɔ:dʒd]	stuffed full of s. th.
	to languish	to become increasingly weaker, *(verkümmern)*
	stunted	prevented from fully growing
	imperceptibly	in a way that can hardly be noticed
	aeon ['i:ən]	an immeasurable period of time
	recapitulated aeons	a reference to the fact that the various stages of the embryo’s development seem to repeat human evolutionary development
	dynamo	a machine that produces electricity
	pint	0.568 of a litre
	to pasteurize ['pɑ:stʃəraɪz]	to rapidly heat and cool s. th. to kill harmful bacteria
	successive	coming one after the other
	layer	*Schicht*
151	**sociability**	the proper behaviour for getting along socially with other people
	toddler ['tɒdlə]	a young child between the ages of one and two and a half
	hunt-the-slipper	a circle game in which players try ot pass a slipper *(Pantoffel)* from one to another without being discovered by the player who is in the middle

	blithe [blaɪð]	happy and unworried	
	to crack a joke	to make a joke	*122*
	severity [sɪ'verətɪ]	strictness, sternness, firmness	
	a public example	the punishing of a person in public to serve as a warning to others	
	eminence ['emɪnəns]	superiority, being well known for s. th.	
	to lead astray [ə'streɪ]	to lead s. o. from the correct or expected way, to cause s. o. to act immorally	
	dispassionately [dɪ'spæʃənətlɪ]	impartially, without being influenced by emotions	
	offence	crime, breaking of a law or rule	
	heinous ['heɪnəs]	wicked, shameful	
	with the greatest ease [i:z]	very easily	
	veneer [və'nɪə]	(fig.) thin outer covering	
152	**jaunty** ['dʒɔ:ntɪ]	cheerful, confident	
	squeak [skwi:k]	a sound like that made by a mouse	
	portentously [pɔ:'tentəslɪ]	in a way showing that s. th. unpleasant is soon to happen	
	serpent ['--]	snake (The Director is compard with a serpent because of how he pronounces the "s".)	
	labours	various tasks	*123*
	to constrain	to force, to oblige, to limit your freedom to act	
	colleague ['kɒli:g]	s. o. who works in the same place	
	to anticipate	to say or do s. th. before the proper time	
	grossly ['grəʊslɪ]	in a way that is obvious to everyone	
	heretical	(relig.) not according to the correct dogma	
	like a babe in a bottle	i. e. like infants	
	subverter	s. o. who tries to destroy the authority of the state	
	conspirator	a person who makes secret plans with others to do s. th. wrong	
	to dismiss	to fire, to remove from a position	
	ignominy ['ɪgnəmɪnɪ]	shame, disgrace	
	forthwith	immediately, at once	
153	**far … removed from**	far away from	
	unfordly	*BNW*'s version of "ungodly"	
	to execute	to carry out	
	to pass judgement upon	to announce a court's decision	
	taken aback	shocked by s. th. unexpected	
	bloated	unpleasantly swollen	
	coquettishly [kɒ'ketɪʃlɪ]	in a flirting manner, in a way meant to attract men	
	undulation	wavelike movement	
	haunch [hɔ:ntʃ]	(usu. in reference to an animal) hips	
	progressively	increasingly	*124*
	in face of	when confronted with	
	petrified ['petrɪfaɪd]	"turned to stone" with fear, etc. *(versteinert)*	
154	**to titter** ['tɪtə]	to giggle, to laugh quietly in a silly way	
	to trail	to be dragged along behind	
	irrepressible	too forceful to stop	
	practical joke	a trick played on s. o. to amuse others	

	to disengage	to separate	
	drowned …	here: made it impossible to hear …	
	uproar	noise made by an excited crowd	
	appalling hush	horrible silence	
	to float	to move about	
	outraged	shocked and angry	
	to stride (strode, stridden)	to walk with long steps	
	connotation	an additional meaning of a word other than its main meaning	
155	**at one remove from**	a step further away from	
	loathsomeness ['ləʊθsəmnɪs]	the quality of being disgusting or shocking	
	moral obliquity [ə'blɪkwətɪ]	immoral behaviour	
	scatalogical	mildly obscene, vulgar	*125*
	impropriety [ˌɪmprə'praɪətɪ]	an improper or indecent word or act	
	to relieve	to lessen	
	peal [pi:l]	loud burst (of laughter)	
	whooping ['hu:pɪŋ]	loud cries of excitement	
	disintegration	the process of breaking up into pieces	
	bewildered	confused	
	humiliation	public shame *(Demütigung)*	

1. Describe the effect of the first four paragraphs of this chapter.
2. What techniques does Huxley use to bring this chapter to a hilarious climax?

156 Chapter Eleven *126*

	to flop	to fall in a heavy, loose way	
	… cut no ice	(coll.) failed to make an impression	
	… was past a joke	went too far to be a joke	
	quaint [kweɪnt]	odd in an attractive old-fashioned way	
	fit	a short attack of an illness	
	to vomit ['vɒmɪt]	to throw up one's food *(sich erbrechen)*	
	intrinsically [ɪn'trɪnsɪklɪ]	in itself	
157	**to clamour** ['klæmə]	to loudly demand s. th.	
	Dr Shaw	probably from George Bernard Shaw, see page 39/*31*	
	to demur [dɪ'mɜ:]	to disapprove, to object	
	to finish s. o. off	to kill, to destroy	
	to confide	to tell personal matters to a person	
	respiratory centre	the part of the brain that controls breathing	
	to rejuvenate [-'---]	to make young again	*127*
	to raise objections	to protest, to make statements of disapproval	
	duration	time during which s. th. lasts	
	Eternity … eyes …	Shakespeare's *Antony and Cleopatra,* I, iii (Cleopatra speaking to Antony – a man torn between duty and love)	

	to pop off	(coll.) to leave suddenly without telling anyone	
	to persist	to continue with s.th. in spite of opposition	
	thenceforward	(form.) from that time on	
158	**patchouli** ['pætʃʊlɪ]	a perfume made from the leaves of a tree found in Asia	
	sonorous ['sɒnərəs]	with a pleasantly full and loud sound	
	to palpitate ['pælpɪteɪt]	to beat rapidly	
	inevitable windings ['waɪndɪŋ]	curves, bends that have to lead to a certain point	
	conviction	firmly held belief or opinion, certainty	
	all-singing feely	parody of a musical film	
	accredited	official, certified	*128*
	guardian	person officially made responsible for another person	
	outstanding	exceptional	
	gibe [dʒaɪb]	mocking remark	
	to cadge [kædʒ]	to get by begging	
159	**deputy** ['depjʊtɪ]	second-in-charge	
	general	person with the highest authority	
	dean [di:n]	*Dekan*	
	Westminster Community Singery	*BNW*'s version of Westminster Abbey in London	
	notability	famous or important person	
	interminable [ɪn'tɜ:mɪnəbl]	seemingly endless	
	inclination	desire, preference	
	in a huff [hʌf]	angry, in a bad mood	
	fizzily	like a fizzy *(prickelnd)* alcoholic drink	
	in the process	at the same time	
	to reconcile ['rekənsaɪl]	to cause s.o. to accept s.th. that was previously unpleasant	
	intoxicant	drug that supresses mental control of one's feelings and actions, e.g. alcohol	
	to forgo	to do without	*129*
	to heighten	to increase	
160	**to pay court to**	to treat s.o. with great respect, like royalty	
	to parade	to display, to show off	
	carping	complaining continuously	
	the more … in that	even more … because	
	elation [ɪ'leɪʃn]	joy and pride	
	captive balloon	a balloon filled with lighter-than-air gas, and tied to the ground with a rope	
	the said …	the particular … (used especially in legal documents)	
	Station Master	person in charge of a station	
	Dravidian	of the original race of people living in the southern part of India	
	porthole	a small round window in the side of a ship or airplane	
	… girdle … minutes	In Shakespeare's *A Midsummer Night's Dream*, II, i, Puck (not Ariel) says to Oberon: "I'll put a girdle round the earth In forty minutes."	

	Ariel ['eərɪəl]	a spirit that was Prospero's servant in *The Tempest*	
	girdle	belt	
161	**awe**	a feeling of respect combined with wonder and fear	*130*
	focussed on	concentrated on	
	entity ['---]	something that has its own existence	
	to skip	to leave out	
	infantility [ˌ--'---]	the quality of being an infant	
	to give place to	to be replaced by	
	mirth [mɜ:θ]	merriment, hearty laughter	
	to lecture	to speak like a professor or university lecturer giving a public talk to students	
	lighting-set	the system of electric lights	
	circular letter	letter sent to several people	
	letter of recommendation	*Empfehlungsschreiben*	
	Human Element	i. e. personnel (the people employed)	
162	**to cold-press**	to give metal a shape by using pressure but no heat	
	four-spindle chucking machine	*vierspindlige Drehbank mit einer Spannvorrichtung*	
	aquiline ['ækwɪlaɪn]	having a hooked nose like an eagle	
	ginger	with reddish-brown hair	
	Senegalese [ˌsenɪgə'li:z]	native of Senegal, a country in West Africa	
	foundry	a place where metal is melted and cooled into different shapes	
	sandy	with reddish-yellow hair	*131*
	pelvis	part of the body between the hips *(Becken)*	
	to cut	here: to make with cutting instruments	
	snubs	i. e. people with snub (short and flat) noses	
	hooks	i. e. people with hooked noses	
	receding ... chins	i. e. people whose chins were backward-sloping	
	prognathous [prɒg'neɪθəs]	sticking out	
	crate	a large box or container, usually made of wood	
	flaxen	with pale yellow hair	
	freckled	with light brown spots on the skin	
	malice ['mælɪs]	desire to harm; here: unpleasant trick	
	to retch [retʃ]	to vomit	
	laurel	*Lorbeerbaum*	
	air pocket	change in air-currents that causes a plane to drop suddenly	
163	**distressed**	much troubled, upset	
	it is worthy of note	(form.) it deserves to be mentioned	
	to run counter	to act in the opposite way	
	to recoil from [rɪ'kɔɪl]	to draw back in disgust or fear	
	Eton ['i:tən]	the largest and most famous of the English elite "public schools", founded by Henry VI in 1440. Huxley himself attended Eton from 1908–1911, and taught there from 1917–1919.	

	Upper School	the building for those in the last year before going on to university (actually exists, built 1694)	
	Lupton's Tower	actually exists, named after Roger Lupton, provost of Eaton from 1504–1535	
	College	actually exists as a building for the lower school	
	Community Singery	*BNW*'s name for the College Chapel, built in the 15th century	
	reared …	lifted, raised up; usu.: reared their ugly heads	
	venerable ['venərəbl]	worthy of respect because of age or character	
	ferro-conrete	*Eisenbeton*	
	vita-glass ['vaɪtə]	a trademark for a special kind of glass that lets ultraviolet rays through	
	quadrangle	four-sided courtyard with buildings round it	
	stature of Our Ford	The real Eton has a statue of Henry VI here.	
	Gaffney	When Huxley was at Eton, there was a School Clerk of this name.	*132*
	Provost	head of a school	
	Miss Keate … headmistress	is probably an allusion to Dr John Keate, headmaster of Eton from 1809 to 1834. He was a renowned classical scholar and a strict disciplinarian, even using the whip.	
	apprehensively	fearfully, anxiously	
	to take a fancy to	to begin to like	
	to jerk	to move with a short sudden action	
164	**a trifle** ['traɪfl]	rather	
	elementary relativity	a basic introduction to Albert Einstein's (1879–1955) Theory of Relativity (which had become accepted among scientists in the years before *BNW* was written, but was still controversial)	
	to think better of s. th.	to decide against doing s. th. after thinking about it	
	As you were.	instruction typical of a military drill: Take a short break.	
	owing to	because of	
	Penitentes	(Span.) here: the group of Spanish-influenced Pueblo Indians John belonged to; in reality, a religious group among the Spanish colonists of North America who believed that suffering (e.g. whipping themselves) was a way of purifying the soul.	
	to prostrate oneself	to lie face downwards	
	Etonian [-'---]	a person attending Eton	
	to strip off	to remove	*133*
	garment	article of clothing	
	redoubled	increased greatly	
	amplified	electronically increased in loudness	
165	**cinematographic** [ˌ----'--]	having to do with films; here: caused by showing a film	
	to embolden	to give s. o. the courage to do s. th.	
	it yielded	i. e. she allowed him to put his arm round her waist	

	willowily ['wɪləʊlɪ]	gracefully, like a willow tree *(Weide)*	
	to snatch	to quickly get s. th.	
	pinch	*Kneifen*	
	shutters	wooden or metal covers to shut out the light of a window	
	pigeon-holed	categorized by placing in a set of small boxes on a wall	
	selenium cell [sɪ'li:nɪəm]	device which can convert light into a current	
	book of reference	book which is consulted for information, e. g. an encyclopedia	
	to indulge in	to allow oneself to do. s. th. enjoyable	
	solitary ['---]	done alone	
	embracement	holding in one's arms	
166	**a matter of course**	s. th. completely normal	*134*
	Savoy [sə'vɔɪ]	a luxurious hotel in London	
	Brentford ['brentfəd]	a suburb of London on the Thames, 8 km west of the city centre	
	stature	a person's height	
	between them	i. e. to be found in this group	
	booking clerk [klɑ:k]	person who sells tickets at a railway station	
	cardboard	made of stiff thick paper	
	caterpillar	here: queue, which moves like a caterpillar *(Raupe)*	
	casket ['kɑ:skɪt]	here: a small box to keep valuable things in	
	What's in those caskets?	an allusion to Shakespeare's *The Merchant of Venice,* I, ii, II, i, III, ii (Portia's dead father had required that she present all those who wanted to marry her with a silver, gold, and lead casket. The one who chose the lead casket could marry her.)	
	to masticate ['mæstɪkeɪt]	to chew	
	affectionately	in a way showing fondness	
167	**engagement**	appointment	
	Young Women's Fordian Association	a parody of the Young Women's Christian Association, founded in the mid 19th century in England	*135*
	Feelytone News	an allusion to Movietone News, the first British sound newsreel, from 1929 on. (Before television people often went to the cinema to see the news on film.)	
	flattering	good for one's prestige or one's self-image *(schmeichelhaft)*	
	conspicuous	noticeable, attracting attention	
	Ford Chief-Justice	*BNW*'s version of the Lord Chief Justice, the highest judge in the British system of courts	
	Arch-Community Songster of Canterbury	*BNW*'s version of the Archbishop of Canterbury, the religious head of the Church of England	
	perpetually	continuously	
	Deauville ['dəʊvi:l]	a seaside resort in northwest France	

	to confess	to admit
	on false pretences	using actions that are intended to deceive people
168	**to make … out**	to understand
	to scent	to put perfume on
	dab [dæb]	here: the act of putting a small amount of s. th. on your skin
	to hug [hʌg]	to hold s. o. tightly as a sign of love *136*
	coma ['kəʊmə]	the state of being in a deep unnatural sleep
	snuggly	loveable, wonderful to hug
	bunny	pet name for a rabbit, here: … for a boyfriend or girlfriend. (The bunny hug was a popular dance at the beginning of the 20th century.)
	herbal ['hɜ:bl]	composed of herbs *(Kräuter)*
	capriccio [kə'prɪtʃɪˌəʊ]	a lively piece of music without a special form.
	rippling	moving like little waves
	arpeggio [ɑ:'pedʒɪəʊ]	(mus.) the notes of a chord played one after the other in upward or downward order
	thyme [taɪm] **… tarragon**	names of herbs used in cooking *(Thymian, Lavendel, Rosmarin, Basilikum, Myrte, Estragon)*
	modulation	(mus.) a change of key *(Tonart)*
	spice	s. th. used to give food a stronger taste (e. g. pepper, paprika) *(Gewürz)*
	ambergris ['æmbəgri:s]	a substance from wales used in perfumes
	camphor ['kæmfə]	substance used to keep moths away *(Kampfer)*
	cedar ['si:də]	*Zedernholz*
	new-mown	freshly cut
	subtle ['sʌtl]	delicate, not easy to notice
	discord	(mus.) dissonance, opp. of harmony
	whiff [wɪf]	slight smell
	kidney pudding	a kind of sausage made of kidney *(Nierenpastete)*
	suspicion	here: slight trace
	dung	manure *(Mist)*
	aromatic	a plant or drug that gives off a pleasant smell
	blast [blɑ:st]	here: sudden strong sound
	round	a general outburst
169	**hyper-violin** ['haɪpə]	an instrument which is "more than" the normal one. This and the other (fictional) instruments suggest the synthesizer, which had not yet been invented at the time of writing.
	languor ['læŋgə]	feeling of dreaming, peacefulness and tender sadness
	bar	(mus.) rhythmic unit *(Takt)*
	to warble	to sing like a bird *(trällern)*
	throaty	from deep in the throat
	hollow ['hɒləʊ]	weak and soft
	charged	filled
	harmonics	overtones
	Gaspard Foster	Huxley is probably referring to Kaspar Förster (1617–1673) German composer, Kapellmeister,

		and singer who was known for having an amazing voice range from high tenor to low bass.
	record	here: s. th. that has never been done before
	to trill	*trillern*
	bat	*Fledermaus* (bats produce very high sounds)
	Ducal	having to do with a Duke *(Herzog)*
	Parma	city in northern Italy that was famous for its opera house in the 18th century
	Lucrezia Ajugari	correct would be Agujari (1743–1783), famous Italian coloratura soprano, whom Mozart really did hear in Parma in 1770.
	to give utterance	here: to give forth, to express
	stall	here: seat near the stage or screen
	fiery ['faɪərɪ]	like fire in colour and brightness
	Three Weeks in a Helicopter	an allusion to Elinor Glyn's novel *Three Weeks* (1907) which includes a famous love-scene on a bearskin rug (cf. p. 48/*38*).
	stereoscopic	three-dimensional in effect (cf. stereophonic)
	to synchronize	to cause to happen at the same time as s. th. else
	to dazzle	to fill with wonder and amazement *137*
	titillation	pleasant thrill or excitement caused by touching
170	**expiringly**	breathing out
	facial	of the face
	erogenous zone	a part of the body that sexually excites
	to tingle	to have a slight stinging feeling in the skin
	twinge	sudden sharp pain
	concussion	damage to the brain caused by a heavy blow
	to knock into a cocked hat	(coll.) to ruin or destroy completely
	assault	violent and sudden attack
	to ravish	to seize with violence, to rape
	tête-à-tête	(Fr.) being together in private
	aerial ['eərɪəl]	happening in the air
	acrobacy ['----]	acrobatics, the skill of doing tricks with the body
	to pack s. o. off	to send away quickly to avoid trouble
	decorously ['dekərəslɪ]	showing proper respect for the manners and customs of society
	mistress	woman who has a steady (though – in our society – illicit) sexual relationship with a man
	gardenia [gɑː'diːnɪə]	a flower
	blare	a vey loud burst of sound
171	**moth**	winged insect that flies by night *(Nachtfalter)*
	feebly	weakly
	to trace	to draw, to imprint, to make an outline
	dewily ['djuːɪlɪ]	as if filled with dew *(Tau)*
	queen's ransom ['rænsəm]	a very large amount of money or valuables (ransom = *Lösegeld)*
	to disengage	to let loose, to remove
	obscurely	in a strange way
	to make haste	to act quickly, to hurry

base	having no moral principles ("Base" and "ignoble" were adjectives in common use at the time of Shakespeare.)
ignoble [ɪg'nəʊbl]	dishonourable
taxicopter	helicopter used as a taxi
vow [vaʊ]	a solemn promise
to run	here: to exist, to be valid
to pluck	*zupfen*
taut [tɔ:t]	tightly stretched
172 **exultantly**	full of delight and pleasure
puff [pʌf]	a small piece of soft material for putting powder on the face
strangled	as if unable to breathe properly 139
to wheel round	to turn round facing the opposite direction
fore-shortened	seeming to be shortened (because of the angle of view)
mouse-nibbled	tiny pieces of which had been eaten by mice
religious	here: exact, precise
173 **Othello**	a play by Shakespeare (Othello is a Moor who kills his fair-haired wife Desdemona out of jealousy.)
affliction	suffering, distress
cupped	formed like a cup

1. In what way has Bernard's attitude to society changed? Explain the change.
2. Explain John's reaction after visiting the factory.
3. What function does Eton have in Brave New World? Discuss the elements of satire.
4. What artistic achievements of Brave New World are mentioned? Discuss how their culture is in some ways more trivial, but in some ways more advanced than ours.
5. Comment on the misunderstandings that arise between Linda and John.

174 Chapter Twelve 140

muffled ['mʌfld]	not very clear because s.th. is in the way
to bellow	to shout angrily
to wheedle	to try to obtain s.th. by being pleasant or flattering
to bawl [bɔ:l]	to cry loudly
exasperated	greatly irritated or annoyed
Ai yaa tákwa!	does not make sense in Zuñi (EJL)
Háni!	does not make sense as a Zuñi insult: "Young brother or sister" (EJL)
ferocity [fə'rɒsətɪ]	fierceness, violence
Sons éso tse-ná.	does not make complete sense in Zuñi: "we will/must ..." (rest unintelligible) (EJL)
to slink back	to move away quietly because of being ashamed
diminished	here: no longer as important as before

	assembly	group of people who have come together	
175	**unsavoury** [ˌʌn'seɪvərɪ]	offensive, not respectable	
	heretical [-'---]	unorthodox, conflicting with accepted beliefs	
	to be had	to be tricked, to be deceived; or: to have had sex with s. o.	*141*
	wretched ['retʃɪd]	miserable, very bad	
	outrage ['--]	s. th. shocking or scandalous	
	scathing ['skeɪðɪŋ]	harsh and severe in one's criticism	
	unwonted [ʌn'wəʊntɪd]	not usual	
	exultation	great happiness	
	apprehension	anxiety, feeling that s. th. terrible is going to happen	
	nausea ['nɔ:sɪə]	feeling of sickness	
176	**thick**	intolerable, beyond what is reasonable	
	crematoria [ˌ--'---]	pl. of "crematorium"	
	reclamation	recovery of waste, recycling	
	pierced	here: very hurt	*142*
	tight	i. e. airtight	
	distraught [dɪ'strɔ:t]	troubled with grief and worry	
	incoherent [ˌɪŋkəʊ'hɪərənt]	unconnected, without a logical order	
	carotine ['kærəˌti:n]	(usu.: carotene) a chemical that gives carrots their orange colour. It is converted into vitamin A by the liver in the body.	
	paté ['pæteɪ]	(Fr.) a paste usually made of meat, liver, vegetables, etc. *(Pastete)*	
	waistcoat	short sleeveless jacket, part of a three-piece suit *(Weste)*	
	crumb [krʌm]	small piece of bread or cake that falls off	
	collation [kɒ'leɪʃən]	a light informal meal; (in the Roman Catholic Church: a small meal that is permitted while fasting)	
	to intercept	to manage to meet or stop s. o. who is moving	
177	**fastening**	device for closing a garment *(Verschluß)*	
	memento	souvenir	
	Diocesan [daɪ'ɒsɪsn]	of a diocese ['daɪəsəs], the area in the charge of (usu.) a bishop	
	dignitary	person of high official position	
	to plead [pli:d]	to ask urgently	
	sepulchral [sɪ'pʌlkrəl]	sounding gloomy as if coming from the grave	*143*
	to mend one's ways	to improve one's behaviour	
	insensible of …	not noticing …	
	elation	joy	
	to puncture	to make a small hole with s. th. sharp in a tyre or balloon, letting out the air (here fig.)	
	to deflate	to let the air out of a balloon, etc. (here fig.)	
178	**novel** ['nɒvl]	original, completely new	
	Marine	having to do with oceans and seas	
	St Helena [ˌsentɪ'li:nə]	an island in the southeast Atlantic, scene of Napoleon's exile and death	
	unsettled	unstable, easily upset	

	Sovereign Good ['sɒvrɪn]	highest goal	
	to take to	to develop a liking for	
179	**to refine**	to make more perfect or pure	*144*
	admissible	allowable, acceptable	
	rapture ['ræptʃə]	great delight or joy	
	declaiming to vacancy	speaking to a non-existent audience	
	O ... too dear ...	from Shakespeare's *Romeo and Juliet,* I, v (when Romeo sees Juliet for the first time)	
	doth [dʌθ]	(arch.) does	
	torch [tɔ:tʃ]	*Fackel*	
	Ethiop	(arch.) a person from Ethiopia	
	sportively	playfully	
	intoxication	feeling of great joy, as if drunk	
	sober ['səʊbə]	here: solemn, serious	
	balloon	i. e. fame and success	
180	**plaintive** ['pleɪntɪv]	sad	
	upon so slight a provocation	because of s. th. insignificant	*145*
	to nourish ['nʌrɪʃ] **a grievance**	here: to keep one's anger or resentment alive	
	to wreak upon [ri:k]	to carry out (a hostile act)	
	accessible	available, easy to reach	
	to inflict upon	to force s. th. unpleasant on s. o.	
	discomfited	confused, embarrassed	
181	**reproach**	words of blame *(Vorwurf)*	
	magnanimity [ˌmægnə'nɪmətɪ]	great generosity of feeling	
	estrangement	state of no longer being friends	
	consolation	comfort in a time of suffering	*146*
	outcry ['-ˌ-]	strong public protest	
	Principal	head of a school	
	... had me up	... summoned me to his office	
	to hand s. o. the sack	to fire s. o.	
	a marked man	a man who is known to have done s. th. wrong and must expect punishment	
182	**dumb** [dʌm]	silent	
	littered	with paper, wrappings, bottles, etc. lying about	
	to rejoice	to feel great joy	
	Egeria [-'---]	girl named after the mythical adviser of Numa, legendary second king of Rome	
	respective	of each person just named	
	posterior [pɒ'stɪərɪə]	the part of the body one sits on	
	essence	the real or inner nature of a thing	*147*
	to populate	to live in, inhabit	
	flatly	completely	
183	**latent** ['leɪtnt]	existing but not yet active	
	pang [pæŋ]	sudden painful emotion	
	alternately [-'---]	first one then the other	
	odious ['əʊdɪəs]	hateful	

	Let the bird …	from Shakespeare's allegorical poem "The Phoenix ['fi:nɪks] and the Turtle" which refers to the love of the phoenix for the turtle (i. e. turtledove) and ends with some verses celebrating spiritual as opposed to physical union. (The Savage goes on to quote from verses 1-4, 10-11 of this poem.)	*148*
	loudest lay	loudest song	
	Arabian	The phoenix was thought to come from Arabia.	
	herald	person or thing that announces s. th.	
	thou [ðaʊ]	(arch.) you	
	harbinger ['hɑ:bɪndʒə]	person or thing that announces s. th. is going to happen	
	fowl [faʊl]	bird	
	tyrant wing	i. e. that dominates over other animals or eats them for food	
	defunctive	of or for the dead	
184	**Property … together …**	from verses 10 and 11 of "The Phoenix and the Turtle"	
	property	here: right of ownership	
	appall'd [ə'pɔ:ld]	here: (arch.) made pale or weak	
	confounded	confused	
	vengeance ['vendʒəns]	revenge	
	defilement	destroying the pureness of s. th.	
	crystal	a clear, transparent mineral or glass; here: example of pure beauty	
	orchard	field with fruit trees	
185	**to resume**	to begin again	*149*
	Capulet and Lady Capulet ['kæpjʊlət]	Juliet's parents in *Romeo and Juliet.*	
	to bully ['bʊlɪ]	to try to get what one wants by frightening s. o.	
	pathetically	causing you to feel pity and sadness	
	to mime [maɪm]	to act using facial expressions and gestures	
	Is there … lies	*Romeo and Juliet,* III, v (what Juliet says in reply to her parents' demand that she marry Paris)	
	bridal bed ['braɪdl]	marriage bed	
	dim monument	i. e. grave	
	Tybalt	a member of the opposing family, killed by Romeo (to whom Juliet was aleady secretly married) with some justification	
	to guffaw [gə'fɔ:]	to laugh loudly	
	hilarity	great amusement	
	anguish	agony, great pain and suffering	
	quenchlessly	here: unable to stop	
	outrage	great anger	
	his pearl from before swine	biblical reference: "Do not cast pearls to swine." Matthew 7:6, i. e. Don't present beauty to someone who has no understanding of it.	
186	**excruciating**	intense, agonizing, extreme	
	X-rayish	like an X-ray *(Röntgenstrahl)*	
	to keep a straight face	to keep oneself from laughing	*150*

	to wince [wɪns]	to move back suddenly with a twisted face when confronted with s. th. unpleasant	

1. How does the Savage's refusal to come to the party affect the various characters?
2. What purpose does the shift of scenes between Lenina, Mustapha, Mond, John, and Bernard serve?
3. Comment on the official Brave New World attitude to science.
4. Try to explain Helmholtz's various reactions to John's readings from Shakespeare, especially from *Romeo and Juliet*?

187 Chapter Thirteen

	to loom up [lu:m]	to come into sight (out of darkness, etc.) with a threatening appearance	
	to detect	to notice	
	pallor ['pælə]	unhealthy paleness	
	glaze	shiny surface	
	lupus	see page 31/*25*	
	A doctor...away.	a *BNW* variation on the saying: "An apple a day keeps the doctor away."	
	jim-jams	feeling of extreme nervousness, the jitters	
	to drive s. th. home	to make s. th. absolutely clear to s. o. by special emphasis	
	adage ['ædɪdʒ]	an old wise saying	
	V.P.S.	Violent Passion Surrogate (see page 175/*141*)	
188	**Mwanza-Mwanza**	There are places called Mwanza in Malawi, Tanzania, and Zaire (all Africa).	*152*
	trypanosomiasis [ˌtrɪpənəsə'maɪəsɪs]	a kind of sleeping-sickness caused by a parasite transmitted by an insect	
	to persevere	to continue trying in spite of difficulties	
	prescription	treatment ordered by a doctor (here fig.: suggestion for solving a problem)	
	perseverence [--'--]	continuous effort to do s. th. in spite of difficulties	
189	**to take a firm line**	to deal with a problem in a firm way	
	Y.W.F.A.	Young Women's Fordian Association (see page 167/*135*)	
	to postpone his confidences	to delay telling his secrets	*153*
	premonition	feeling that s. th. is going to happen	
	satin ['sætɪn]	a shiny cloth usually made of silk	
	rakishly ['reɪkɪʃlɪ]	in a way meant to look casual and confident	
	tilted	here: pulled down to one side	
190	**reverently**	in a way showing respect and admiration	
	Admired ... creature's best.	cf. *The Tempest*, III, i where Ferdinand praises Miranda's beauty ("Admir'd Miranda! ...").	
	tenderness	warm feeling, affection	
	peerless ['pɪələs]	without equal	
	clumsy	moving in a careless or awkward way	

	oaf [əʊf]	stupid, ungraceful person
	to snap	to say quickly in an angry manner
191	**There be … sets off. … some kinds … undergone.**	cf. *The Tempest,* III, i: Ferdinand has been ordered to pile up some heavy logs of wood by Prospero, Miranda's father, as a way of testing his love for his daughter.
	there be … are	(subjunctive form, arch.) there may be … which are
	baseness	here: dirty work
	nobly	unselfishly, generously
	emblem	sign (i. e. Lenina's blushing as a sign of her feelings)
	tide	usu.: the rise and fall of the sea caused by the pull of the moon; here: sudden flow of emotion
192	**Outliving … decays.**	Shakespeare's *Troilus and Cressida,* III, ii *155* (Troilus speaking to Cressida – he will be disappointed about Cressida later in the play)
	to outlive	to last longer than
	outward	here: (n.) outward appearance
	swifter	faster
	to decay [dɪ'keɪ]	to lose strength, to rot
	If thou … rite …	*The Tempest,* IV, i (Prospero telling Ferdinand that he may not have sex with Miranda until they are properly married)
	virgin ['--]	untouched, pure, i. e. never having had sex
	sanctimonious [ˌsæŋktɪ'məʊnɪəs]	holy
	exasperation	extreme annoyance with loss of patience
	to drivel away ['drɪvl]	to talk nonsense
	blackamoor	a person with dark skin
	The murkiest … lust	*The Tempest,* IV, i (Ferdinand promising not to give in to temptation)
	murky	gloomy, dark
	den	cave, hole, etc., as the home of a wild animal
	opportune ['ɒpətju:n]	suitable
193	**our worser genius**	(arch.) the badness in us, the evil part of us
	can	(arch.) is able to make
	lust	sexual desire *(Wollust)*
	untwined	removed her arms that were tightly round him
	to unbuckle	to open a buckle (fastening of a belt) *156*
	to rip	to tear quickly; here: to open quickly by pulling the zipper
	hem	lower end of a garment *(Saum)*
	to condense	(of a gas) to become a solid or liquid (here fig.)
	a too, too solid certainty	allusion to *Hamlet* I, ii: "O that this too, too solid flesh would melt …" (Mourning his father's death, and upset about his mother's speedy remarriage, Hamlet wishes he were dead, too.)
	bell-bottomed trousers	trousers wider at the bottom, as worn by sailors

	shell pink	the colour of sea-shells *(Muscheln)*
	to dangle	to hang loosely
	For those milk paps … eyes …	Shakespeare's *Timon of Athens,* IV, 3 (where Timon tells soldiers not to show any pity even for children, and not let the sight of a young woman's breasts make them weak)
	milk pap [pæp]	nipple of the breast
	window bars	(arch.) a kind of corset supporting the breasts
	to bore at	to pierce
	alluring	attractive, charming, fascinating
	to drill	to pierce, to bore
	resolution	determination to keep to one's decision
	The strongest … or else …	*The Tempest,* IV, i (Prospero warning Ferdinand that sexual passion can easily cause one to break a promise)
	oath	solemn promise *(Schwur, Eid)*
	abstemious	moderate, holding back on pleasure
	wriggle ['rɪgl]	twisting movement
194	**to flap**	to move up and down
	intruding	entering or coming without being asked or wanted
	to bring to bay	to force a fleeing animal or person into a position from which there is no escape
	spell	words that have magic power
	distorted	twisted *157*
	to twitch	to make sudden, small, nervous movements
	aghast [ə'gɑ:st]	horrified, filled with horror
	whore [hɔ:]	prostitute
	Impudent strumpet …	*Othello,* IV, ii (Othello wrongly accusing his wife of being unfaithful)
	impudent ['ɪmpjʊdənt]	without shame
	strumpet	whore, prostitute
195	**to stagger**	to walk with difficulty, almost falling
	to clench	to close tightly
	to crouch [kraʊtʃ]	to lower the body by bending the knees
	to make a dash for	to run quickly to
	prodigious [prə'dɪdʒəs]	powerful
	to bound	to move along quickly with jumping movements
	leisure ['leʒə]	here: enough time
	to take stock of s. th.	to consider or examine s. th. carefully before taking action
	imprint	mark
	gingerly	cautiously
	The wren … sight …	Shakespeare's *King Lear,* IV, vi (Lear is here excusing lechery and adultery as harmless in comparison with the way his daughters have treated him.)
	wren [ren]	a small bird *(Zaunkönig)*
	… goes to't …	performs sexual intercourse
	gilded	as if covered with gold
	to lecher ['letʃə]	to have excessive sex

	the fitchew … imagination	*King Lear,* IV, vi (Further on in the same speech Lear is accusing all women of lechery, and is no longer tolerant of it.)	*158*
	fitchew ['fɪtʃu:]	*Stinktier*	
	soiled	(arch.) fed with fresh cut grass (thought to increase sexual desire)	
	riotous ['raɪətəs]	unrestrained	
	Centaur ['sentɔ:]	in Greek mythology a creature that is human above the waist and below the waist a horse	
	girdle ['gɜ:dl]	here: waist	
	But to the girdle … inherit.	The gods only possess the part of the body above the waist.	
	fiend [fi:nd]	devil	
	sulphurous ['sʌlfərəs]	smelling of sulphur *(Schwefel)*	
	to scald [skɔ:ld]	to burn with very hot water	
	stench	strong and unpleasant smell, stink	
	consumption	wasting away, wearing out	
	fie … pah!	expressions of disgust	
196	**civet** ['sɪvɪt]	a fluid used for perfumes found in the body of a catlike animal of the same name that lives in Africa and Asia	
	apothecary [-'----]	a person who mixes and sells medicines	
	to ingratiate [ɪn'greɪʃɪeɪt]	to try to get the favour of s. o. by being very pleasant to this person	
	O thou weed … at it …	*Othello,* IV, ii (some sentences from a speech in which Othello is wrongly accusing his wife of being unfaithful)	
	weed [wi:d]	plant that is troublesome and unwanted	
	thou … art	(arch.) you … are	
	to ache [eɪk]	to be in pain	
	to stop the nose	to close up one's nose	
	defiant [dɪ'faɪənt]	refusing to obey	
	ventilator	here: opening to let air through	
	to pace	to walk with regular steps backwards and forwards	
	The devil … potato finger …	*Troilus and Cressida,* V, ii (spoken by Theresites while secretly watching the faithless Cressida and Diomedes together)	
	luxury	(arch.) lust, lechery	
	rump	the part of the body one sits on	
	potato finger	(arch. sl.) male sex organ (potatoes were thought to increase sexual desire)	
	gruffly	roughly and deeply because of being in a bad mood	
	to tramp	to walk with firm, heay steps	
	to subside	to become less violent	
197	**to parley** ['pɑ:lɪ]	to discuss	
	If I do not … am.	Shakespeare's *Twelfth Night,* I, v (Olivia's answer to Viola's question: "Are you the lady of the house?" an allusion to the many mistaken identities in the play)	*159*
	to usurp [ju:'zɜ:p]	to seize or take over a throne, land, etc. without authority	

	Park Lane	an exclusive area of London	
	infinity	here: great number	
	to peep	to look through a small opening from a hidden place	

1. What is Lenina's "problem"? Why are the normal Brave New World cures not able to help her?
2. How would you explain John's refusal to accept Lenina's advances? Do you think he behaved properly? Does he really love and respect her?
3. Find out more about the context of John's *Othello* quotations. Does John show a real understanding of Shakespeare's play?

198 Chapter Fourteen *160*

	primrose	pale yellow (like the flower)	
	tile	flat squares used to cover walls, etc. *(Kachel)*	
	hearse [hɜ:s]	car, or wagon, etc. used to carry a dead body to the graveyard	
	to whirr [wɜ:]	*surren*	
	presiding [prɪ'zaɪdɪŋ]	in charge	
	ward	large room (or, nowadays, department) in a hospital with a large number of beds	
	galloping	here: progressing at a very fast rate	
	moribund ['mɒrɪbʌnd]	near death	
199	**distress**	great pain, suffering, sorrow	
	unwithered [ʌn'wɪðəd]	without wrinkles, not dried out	
	second infancy	i. e. old age	
	to prop up [prɒp]	to raise and prevent from falling back	
	hither and thither ['hɪðə/'θɪðə]	in various directions, backwards and forewards	
	illumined [ɪ'lu:mɪnd]	usu.: illuminated, i. e. filled with light	
	bloated ['bləʊtɪd]	unpleasantly swollen	
	imbecile ['ɪmbəsi:l]	stupid, with a weak mind	
	antics ['æntɪks]	absurd behaviour	
	vox [vɒks]	(Lat.) voice, sound	
200	**Wurlitzeriana** [ˌ----'--]	presumably a musical form composed for the Wurlitzer Organ, developed by the German-American of the same name in 1880. With its special electronic effects it was frequently used in cinemas to accompany silent films until the early 1930s.	
	rendering	performance, version, interpretation	
	draught [drɑ:ft]	flow (of air)	
	verbena [vɜ:'bi:nə]	a pleasant smelling flower from the tropical areas of North and South America	
	embellished	made more beautiful by adding decorations	
	constituent	part of a whole	
	to go off	here: to die	
	to stoop [stu:p]	to bend the top half of the body down	*162*
	over his childhood	i. e. over him when he was a child	

	to well up	to start to flow	
201	**undefiled** [ˌʌndɪˈfaɪld]	not corrupted	
	between the lot of them	in the whole group	
	puggishly [ˈpʌgɪʃlɪ]	with the face of a pug *(Mops)*	
	goggling [ˈgɒglɪŋ]	wide open and sticking out	
	to clamber [ˈklæmbə]	to climb using the feet and hands	
	taut-skinned [tɔ:t]	smooth skinned, without wrinkles	*163*
	sexagenarian [ˌseksədʒɪˈneərɪən]	a person between 60 and 69 years old	
	flaccid [ˈflæksɪd]	not firm, soft, flabby	
	to pop up	to suddenly appear	
	clear	all the way, completely	
	smart	sharp and quick	
	box on the ears	blow with the hand on the side of s. o.'s head	
	brat [bræt]	badly-behaved child	
	truculently [ˈtrʌkjʊləntlɪ]	defiantly, aggresively	
	reassured	with her confidence back again, no longer feeling anxiety	
	a trifle [ˈtraɪfl]	rather	
	so mind	So watch out!	
	hunt-the-zipper	see page 151/*121* under "hunt-the-slipper"	
203	**to recapture**	here: to bring back	*164*
	resurrection	revival, bringing back to life (fig.)	
	to trickle [ˈtrɪkl]	to flow in a thin stream or in drops	
	strenuous [ˈstrenjʊəs]	needing a great deal of energy and effort	
	denial	refusing to accept the truth of s. th.	
	crescendo	(mus.) gradual increase in loudness	
204	**sublime** [səˈblaɪm]	inspiring admiration, noble, of great spiritual value	
	imminence [ˈɪmɪnəns]	nearness (of a future event)	
	ordure [ˈɔ:djʊə]	dung, animal waste	*165*
	balked [bɔ:kd]	hindered, prevented from doing s. th., frustrated	
	transposed	placed in a new setting	
	to fancy	to imagine, to picture	
	intruder	s. o. entering a place without a right to do so	
	to croak [krəʊk]	to speak hoarsely and with difficulty *(krächzen)*	
205	**to claw** [klɔ:]	to desperately try to seize s. th.	
	irresolute [ɪˈrezəlu:t]	uncertain how to act	*166*
	to enact [ɪˈnækt]	to act out, to perform as if on a stage	
	mischief [ˈmɪstʃɪf]	harm	
206	**to undo**	to remove the effects of s. th., to reverse	
	wholesome	having a good moral effect, good for the body and spirit	
	menaced	here: endangered	
	éclair [ɪˈkleə]	finger-shaped cake filled with cream and covered with chocolate	
	articulate [-ˈ---]	distinct, clear	
	God!	cf. page 142/*114*, where John discovers "Time and Death and God"	
	warbling	continuous background music, like bird-song	

	stump	what remains of s. th. after a larger part has been removed	
	variously	in many different ways	*167*
	butt [bʌt]	the unused end of s. th	

1. Compare the attitude towards death in Brave New World with that of our own society.
2. What seems to be Huxley's attitude? How do you feel about the BNW kind of conditioning?
3. What are John's feelings about his dying mother?

208		**Chapter Fifteen**	*168*
	menial staff ['mi:nɪəl]	those persons doing the unskilled work such as washing, cleaning, etc.	
	dolichocephalic [ˌdɒlɪkəʊsɪ'fælɪk]	with relatively long heads	
	vestibule ['vestɪbju:l]	lobby or entrance hall	
	bursar ['bɜ:sə]	person in charge of the finances of an institution	
	to shoulder	to push with the shoulder	
	to squeak/to growl [graʊl]	here: to speak in a very high-pitched/low-pitched voice	
	train	series, long line of s. th.	
	halo ['heɪləʊ]	a circle of light round a saint's head	
	haloed in orange	with orange-coloured hair	
	beaked [bi:kt]	i. e. with a pointed, hooked nose (like a bird's beak)	
	stubbly	with short stiff hairs (from not shaving that day)	
	nudging	pushing	
	sinking sense of …	feeling that s. th. bad is about to happen	
	to know s. th. for	to realize that s. th. is	
	recurrent	happening again and again	
209	**repentance**	regret for one's bad behaviour *(Reue)*	
	mob [mɒb]	large noisy crowd that can become violent	
	to overtop [ˌ--'-]	to be higher than the surroundings	
	How many … new world …	again from *The Tempest,* V, i	
	jaunty ['dʒɔ:ntɪ]	showing cheerfulness and self-confidence	*169*
	peremptorily [pə'remptrəlɪ]	in a commanding tone	
	to shove [ʃʌv]	to push roughly	
	fiendishly ['fi:ndɪʃlɪ]	like an evil spirit, wickedly, cruelly	
	nauseous ['nɔ:sɪəs]	causing a sick feeling	
210	**to jostle** ['dʒɒsl]	to push s. o. roughly	
	reparation	s. th. done to compensate for a past wrong	
	below his breath	in a whisper	*170*
	Lend me your ears …	i. e. Listen to me! – from Mark Anthony's famous speech in Shakespere's *Julius Caesar,* III, ii (Mark Anthony was much more successful than the Savage: he was able to change the opinion of the crowd.)	

	propitiatingly [prəˈpɪʃɪeɪtɪŋ]	as if trying to please	
	There's a good fellow.	i.e. Thank you for doing what I say; it's nice of you to do so.	
211	**vicious** [ˈvɪʃəs]	savage, dangerous, violent	
	to enfold	to enclose, to cover from all sides	
	the quick	the core, centre, essence	
	to nip across to	to make a short visit (to somewhere nearby)	
	Biarritz [ˈbɪərɪts]	famous French resort on the southwest coast	
	sporticopter	invented word: a "sporty" helicopter	
212	**ardour** [ˈɑːdə]	eagerness, enthusiasm	*171*
	Mewling and puking…	Shakespeare's *As You Like It*, II, vii: the famous "Seven Ages of Man" speech beginning with "All the world's a stage,/And all the men and women merely players…" and then describing the stages of life from infancy to second infancy	
	to mewl [mjuːl]	to cry weakly	
	to puke [pjuːk]	to get sick, to vomit *(kotzen)*	
	exasperated	irritated, angered	
	bestial [ˈbestɪəl]	like a beast, brutish	
	carapace [ˈkærəpeɪs]	hard protective shell of animals such as crabs, tortoise, etc.	
	sullen	in a bad mood	
	compassion	sympathy for the suffering of others, with the desire to help	
	…as it were…	*sozusagen*	
	absorbed into	sucked into	
	manhood	being a man, having the (good) qualities of a man (rather ambiguous: he may mean "humanity")	
	fluent	able to speak smoothly	
	grimly	earnestly, seriously	
	wanton [ˈwɒntən]	done on purpose for no good reason	
	sacrilege [ˈsækrɪlɪdʒ]	treating a holy thing with disrespect	
	Ford helps … themselves.	cf. the actual proverb: God helps them that help themselves. (Benjamin Franklin, 1736)	
213	**exultation**	joy, great happiness	
	to punch [pʌntʃ]	to strike hard with one's fist	*172*
	assailant [əˈseɪlənt]	attacker	
	they're done for	they haven't got a chance, they're finished	
	goggled-eyed	with wide-open eyes that stick out	
	swine-snouted	with a nose like a pig	
	to buckle	to fasten	
	vapour [ˈveɪpə]	a liquid that has been turned to gas	
	charged	loaded, filled	
	anaesthetic [ˌænɪsˈθetɪk]	substance that produces unconsciousness	
	to lay out	here: to knock unconsious	
	squirt by squirt	with each squirt *(Spritze)*	
	ferocious [fəˈrəʊʃəs]	aggressive, violent, fierce	
214	**chatter**	foolish talk	
	to wamble [ˈwɒmbl]	to move with a rolling motion *(schwanken)*	

	tendon	strong fibre connecting bones and muscles *(Sehne)*	
	jelly	a soft, clear substance *(Gallert)*	
	to dim	to make unclear, or less bright	*173*
	comprehensive	here: including everyone	
	Bursary ['bɜ:sərɪ]	bursar's office	
	valediction [ˌvælɪ'dɪkʃn]	act of saying farewell	
	to disperse	to cause a gathering to leave	
	to blubber	to weep noisily	
215	**... Ford keep you.**	refer to Numbers (third Book of Moses) 6:24–26 "The Lord bless thee, and keep thee ..." It is a blessing *(Segnung)* often given at the end of a church service	
	angelic [-'--]	like an angel	
	to anaesthetize [ə'ni:sθətaɪz]	to give s. o. an anaesthetic	
	to dab	to touch lightly	

1. Why does John try to stop the Deltas from getting their soma rations? How successful is he in convincing the Deltas?
2. Compare Helmholtz's behaviour in the crisis with that of Bernard.
3. What kind of "crowd control" is used in Brave New World?

216 ## Chapter Sixteen *175*

to usher	to lead or conduct s. o. into a room, etc.
obscure	here: vague
to deprecate ['deprəkeɪt]	(arch. in this meaning) to try to prevent from happening, often with prayers
wrath [rɒθ]	great anger
inquisitiveness	curiosity
bobbin ['bɒbɪn]	usu.: a small cylinder round which thread is wound *(Spule)*; here: some kind of data storage device
volume ['vɒlju:m]	book
to stamp	to produce a mark on paper, leather, etc. by using pressure
My Life and Work	Henry Ford actually did write an autobiography (with another writer) of the same title in 1923. In it, he was very optimistic about the benefits of mass production.
Detroit	city in Michigan, the centre of the US car industry
Society for the Propagation of Fordian Knowledge	an allusion to the Society for Promoting Christian Knowledge, founded in 1698 by the Church of England. It still exists today. It owns a number of publishing houses and book shops in Great Britain, and helps the Church overseas to publish and distribute Christian literature.

	propagation	spreading beliefs more widely	
217	**to bluster**	to speak loudly and boastfully	
	Sometimes … voices …	*The Tempest,* III, ii (said by Caliban, the monster son of a dead witch)	*176*
	to twangle	to make a sound like a guitar	
	with impunity [ɪmˈpju:nətɪ]	with no unpleasant consequences	
218	**Goats and monkeys!**	*Othello,* IV, i (These animals are associated with lust and trickery. Othello hinself was tricked into believing that his wife was lustful for other men.)	
	vehicle [ˈvɪəkl]	here: a means or medium of expression	
	parenthetically [ˌpærənˈθetɪklɪ]	introduced as an additional thought or explanation	
219	**blissfully ignorant**	happy not to know s.th. (The phrase comes from the poem "Ode on a Distant Prospect of Eton College" by Thomas Gray (1716–1771): "where ignorance is bliss,/'Tis folly to be wise."	*177*
	to plague [pleɪg]	to cause constant suffering or hardship	
	to chuck out	to throw out	
	… told by an idiot …	*Macbeth,* V, v (where Macbeth talks about life having no meaning)	
	distinguished	famous, celebrated	
	ingenuity [ˌɪndʒɪˈnju:ətɪ]	inventive talent, cleverness	*178*
220	**glamour** [ˈglæmə]	charm, fascination, great attractiveness	
	picturesqueness [ˌpɪktʃəˈresknəs]	striking, vivid and expressive quality	
	overthrow	defeat, downfall, destruction	
	midget	extremely small person	
	gyroscope [ˈdʒaɪrəskəʊp]	a device containing a disc rotating on an axis, which is used to stabilize and guide ships, airplanes and rockets	
	unswerving	not turning aside	
	to imply	here: to suggest, to indicate	
	onrush	(fig.) rapid progress	
	oratory [ˈɒrətrɪ]	skill at speaking in public	
	up to synthetic standards	equal to that produced by machines	
	while you're about it	i. e. when you're producing human beings in bottles anyway	
221	**to assume responsibilities**	to take, to accept responsibilities	*179*
	line of least resistance	easiest course of action	
	to be foredoomed	to be destined or condemned to do s. th.	
	fixation	in Freudian psychology: a strong love or attachment to another person or object developed early in life	
	to be confined	to be restricted or limited	
	You cannot pour … bottles.	cf. the saying (of biblical origin, Matt. ix. 17): "You cannot put new wine into old bottles."	

	Cyprus ['saɪprəs]	island in the eastern Mediterranean (a British colony before World War II)	
	to clear	here: to remove, to get rid of	
	to set at naught [nɔ:t]	to ignore, to make ineffectual	
	to be detailed for s. th.	to be given a task to do	
	spell	period of time	
	to intrigue [ɪn'tri:g]	here: to try to gain s. th. by secret means	
	constrained	forced	
	to put s. th. into execution	to carry out, to put into practice	
	to afflict	to cause distress or suffering	
	morsel	small piece of food	
	menace	threat, danger	
	chary of ['tʃeərɪ]	careful, cautious about	
	item	factor, detail	*181*
	incompatible [ˌ--'---]	not able to exist with s. th. else	
	to muzzle	to cover the mouth of a dangerous dog; here fig.: to control, to censor	
	platitude	an obvious statement that says nothing new	
224	**recipe** ['resəpɪ]	directions for preparing food	
	scullion	(arch.) person who does the cleaning and unskilled work in the kitchen	
	illicit	illegal	
	to galvanize	here: to excite, to startle	
	unseemly	not in good taste or style	
	paroxysm ['pærəksɪzəm]	fit, convulsion, sudden attack	
	to grovel ['grɒvl]	to beg for s. th. with a show of shame and humility	*182*
	inexhaustibly	seemingly never coming to an end	
	vaporization	here: treatment with a substance in gas form	
225	**footman**	servant, attendant (usu. in uniform)	
	to regret	here: to regret the loss of s. th.	
	to consult ones preferences	to do what one would really like to do	
	matriarchy ['meɪtrɪɑ:kɪ]	a society in which women have most of the authority	
226	**scope**	the area within which s. o./s. th. can act	
	enquiries [ɪn'kwaɪərɪ]	here: research	*183*
	sedulously ['sedjʊləslɪ]	with great care	
	… go on indefinitely …	a possible allusion to the English writer H. G. Wells (1866–1946), who believed that man could be made perfect through scientific advance, and wrote a number of books in the first two decades of the 20th century to support this view	
	truth and beauty	a possible allusion to a group of intellectuals in the 1920s known as the Bloomsbury group, many of whom were intellectual elitists, believing civilization to be in danger of being destroyed by the masses	
	sovereign ['sɒvrɪn]	here: highest	

to change one's tune — to change one's opinion
227 **lethal chamber** ['li:θl] — a room in which people are executed
Marquesas [mɑ:'keɪsæs] — a group of volcanic islands in the South Pacific, in French Polynesia
Samoa [sə'məʊə] — group of islands in the South Pacific
bracing ['breɪsɪŋ] — refreshing, stimulating
approbation — approval, praise *184*
Falkland Islands [ˌfɔ:lklənd] — a group of islands (British crown colony) in the South Pacific east of Argentina

1. Why does Mustapha Mond believe it is not possible to have real literature and art in Brave New World?
2. How does the Controller explain the impossibility of having a society solely consisting of Alphas? And why was it impossible to reduce low-caste working hours? Can you think of any other solutions to these related problems?
3. What is meant by "real science"? What role does it play in Brave New World?
4. How sympathetically is Mustapha Mond portrayed in this chapter? How convincing are his arguments?

228 **Chapter Seventeen** *185*

... the precipice ... — cf. pp. 114/*92* and 141–142/*114*
to rummage ['rʌmɪdʒ] — to look for s.th. among a lot of other things
The Imitation of Christ — a religious book said to have been written at the beginning of the 15th century by Thomas à Kempis. The book is very mystical in nature and does not trust human intellect.
William James — American psychologist and philosopher (1842–1910), who rejected complicated and abstract systems of philosophy. He preferred "usable" ideas learnt from experience. In *Varieties* (1902) he took the position that any aspect of religious experience was "true" when it provided emotional satisfaction to the individual.
229 **avowed** — openly admitted
Cardinal Newman — John Henry Newman (1801–1890) became a priest in the Church of England and later converted to Roman Catholicism in 1845, becoming one of the most important Catholic theologians of the 19th century. For him the spiritual was more important than the material, and the doctrine of the Church superior to feeling and emotion.
I, Pandulph, ... — Shakespeare's *King John*, III, i (a line spoken by the Pope's representative in England)
Milan — large city in northern Italy (It.: *Milano*, Ger.: *Mailand*)

	Maine de Biran	French statesman and philosopher (1766–1824). He did not agree that knowledge was acquired only from external sense experience, rather he emphasized the importance of the inner self and the will of the individual for finding the basis of morality. He became, much like Huxley himself, increasingly interested in mysticism.	
	A man … heaven and earth …	cf. *Hamlet*, I, v: "There are more things in heaven and earth Horatio, Than are dreamt of in your philosophy." (spoken by Hamlet to his friend Horatio after seeing his father's ghost)	
230	**irksomeness**	s. th. annoying, trouble, bother	
	acknowledgement	here: expression of thanks or appreciation for s. th.	
	reference	here: paying attention to, consideration of	
	A man grows old …	a passage by Biran	
	listlessness	lack of energy or enthusiasm	
	to lull [lʌl]	to calm, to make quiet	*187*
	vain imaginings	worthless thoughts	
	fancy ['fænsɪ]	imagination	
	sensibilities	ability to respond emotionally to impressions	
	to obscure	to make difficult to see and understand	
231	**to leak away**	(fig.) to slowly become lost	
	phenomenal existence	existence as a physical phenomenon, i. e. s. th. that can be noticed by our senses	
	to bolster up	to support, to strengthen	
	to abide	to remain	
	to play s. o. false	to deceive s. o.	
	foolery	foolish behaviour	
	repose	quiet, peace, rest	
	something immovable	here: s. th. constant and unchangeable, i. e. God (the "Prime Mover" in the philosophical system of Aristotle)	
	to manifest ['---]	to show clearly, to reveal	*188*
232	**to do up**	to fasten	
	(Francis Herbert) Bradley	an English philospher (1846–1924) who was opposed to the Utilitarian belief that happiness is the goal of human life	
	the gods … eyes.	*King Lear*, V, iii (spoken by Edgar, the legitimate son of the Earl of Gloucester to his illegitimate half-brother, Edmund, after fatally wounding him in single combat; Edmund had previously been partly responsible for the torture and blinding of their father, Gloucester).	
233	**pleasant vices**	here: their father's adultery, with Edmund's mother	
	vicious place ['vɪʃəs]	i. e. the bed where Gloucester slept with the other woman	*189*
	thee	(arch., object form of "thou") you	
	he got	(arch., bibl.) he fathered	
	… God managing things …	A close examination of *King Lear* will show, if anything, that the gods are not just. It is the innocent who suffer most.	

	'tis	it is	
	mistress	the reference here is to Regan, King Lear's evil daughter, who was Edmund's mistress	
	code of law	legal system	
	in the last resort	in the end, finally	
	Providence	fate, God's plan *(die Vorsehung)*	
	to take one's cue from [kju:]	to get the signal what to do from	
	postulate ['pɒstjʊlət]	s. th. assumed to be true as the basis for an argument	
	But value ... prizer	*Troilus and Cressida,* II, ii (spoken by Hector, the only completely honest character in the play)	
	to dwell	to live (in a place); here: to be a part of	
	estimate ['estɪmət]	the (high) value put on s. th.	
	'tis precious of itself	i. e. it has its own value or worth	
	prizer	the person making a value judgement	
234	**self-denial**	refusing to fulfill one's own desires	*190*
	self-indulgence	allowing oneself everything one desires	
	neurasthenia [ˌnjʊərəs'θi:nɪə]	(a term no longer in scientific use) a nervous condition with the symtoms of tiredness, loss of energy and self-respect	
	divided allegiances [ə'li:dʒənsɪz]	feelings of loyalty to different groups or beliefs	
235	**to reconcile** ['rekənsaɪl]	to make s. o. become friendly again	
	long-sufferring	able to tolerate trouble and bad treatment	
	If after every tempest ... death ...	*Othello,* II, i (spoken by Othello when he is happy to see Desdemona again, and therefore is able to see some good even in quarrel)	*191*
	Mátsaki	a pueblo that no longer exists; it was located 5 km east of Zuñi	
	to hoe	to break up the surface soil and so destroy weeds *(hacken)*	
	Whether 'tis nobler ... them ...	*Hamlet,* III, i (spoken by Hamlet when he's thinking of committing suicide so as to escape from his responsibilities)	
	sling	*Schleuder*	
	outrageous fortune	i. e. the terrible things that might happen	
	to take arms against	(fig.) to defend oneself against	
236	**caress**	gentle stroke, a light touch	
	flabby	not firm, loose because of too much fat	
	Exposing what is mortal ... egg-shell	*Hamlet,* IV, iv (Hamlet is questioning whether one should put oneself in danger for s. th. that is not very important)	
	adrenal	the adrenal gland *(Nebenniere)*	*192*
237	**system**	here: body, organism	
	adrenin	(mistake or misprint) correct: adrenaline, a hormone produced by the adrenal glands that increases the heart rate and stimulates the nervous system	
	tonic ['tɒnɪk]	tending to make one feel happier and healthier	
	Desdemona [--'--]	Othello's wife	

	inconvenience	s.th. that causes trouble or difficulties	
	lousy	infested with lice; or: (coll.): feeling ill	
	apprehension	feeling of fear that s.th. terrible might happen	

1. Why is religion superfluous in Brave New World according to Mustapha Mond? Consider what you have read in previous chapters: Has all "religious sentiment" really been done away with?
2. What arguments does John supply for the right to be unhappy?
3. Who seems to gain the upper hand in the argument in the end? Explain.
4. Of what importance is this chapter for the novel?

238 **Chapter Eighteen** *193*

	solicitously [-'----]	showing concern	
	to purify	to make clean and pure	
	mustard ['mʌstəd]	a yellow paste used to flavour foods *(Senf)*	
239	**to cut s.o. short**	to interrupt s.o. and stop him/her from going on	*194*
240	**down-line/up-line**	air-traffic routes in both directions	
	Guildford ['gɪlfəd], **Godalming …, Farnham** ['fɑ:nəm]	towns and villages between London and Portsmouth on the south coast of England (Huxley himself was born at Godalming, Surrey.)	
	Wey [weɪ]	river that flows through Guildford and Godalming	
	the Hog's Back	a ridge of land between Farnham and Guildford	
	to deflect	to cause to go along another course	
	hermitage	a place where a person can live completely alone	
	crest	top	
	to pacify	to calm, to make peaceful	*195*
	Claudius ['klɔ:dɪəs]	Hamlet's uncle, who killed Hamlet's father to take the throne; he prays for forgiveness in Act III, scene iii.	
	guardian animal	animal believed to protect or guard s.o. (cf. "guardian angel" and p. 110/*88* "totemism")	
	ache [eɪk]	continuous, steady pain	
	excruciating [ɪk'skru:ʃɪeɪtɪŋ]	extreme, causing great pain	
241	**clenched**	tightly pressed together	
	vantage point	position from which one has a good view of a scene	
	incarnation	physical, human form (taken by a spirit) *(Verkörperung)*	
	divine	belonging to or having to do with God	
	to pamper ['pæmpə]	to make too comfortable and happy, to treat too kindly	
	sty [staɪ]	house in which pigs are kept; fig.: dirty place	
	blind	here: hidden	
	to bound	to form the limit or boundary	

	extremity [ɪkˈstremətɪ]	farthest point, end, or edge	
	to twinkle	to shine with an unsteady light, like stars	
	constellation	a group of stars that form an imagined picture	
	plumbless [ˈplʌmləs]	impossible to find the "depth" of	*196*
	modest [ˈmɒdɪst]	not splendid, ordinary	
	poultry farm [ˈpəʊltrɪ]	a farm where chickens, geese, turkeys, etc. are raised	
242	**to intervene**	to come between	
	seductive	very attractive and tempting	
	gorse [gɔ:s]	a prickly bush common in rocky, coastal areas of the British Isles *(Stechginster)*	
	Scotch fir [fɜ:]	also called Scots pine *(Waldkiefer)*	
	birch [bɜ:tʃ]	*Birke*	
	bed of rushes	group of rushes *(Binsen)* growing from the bottom of the pond	
	aridities [əˈrɪdəti:z]	characteristics of a dry climate	
	Surrey [ˈsʌrɪ]	county in southeast England to the southwest of London	
	heath [hi:θ]	*Heidemoorland*	
	links	a piece of land where golf is played	
	fire drill	a primitive device consisting of a stick and a piece of wood used to start a fire	
	starch	a carbohydrate contained in flour, potatoes, etc.	
	pan-glandular	probably: containing vitamins needed by all the body's glands	
	vindictively	showing a desire to hurt	*197*
	to tide s. o. over	to be enough to get s. o. through a difficult period	
	game	wild animals, fish, etc. that are hunted for food	
	water-fowl [faʊl]	birds that can swim in water, e.g. ducks, geese	
	to set to work	to begin to work	
	ash	*Esche*	
	shaft	the long part (of an arrow, etc.)	
	copse [kɒps]	small group of trees growing very close to each other	
	sapling [ˈsæplɪŋ]	young tree	
	to fell	to cut (a tree) down	
	unbranched	with no branches growing out of it	
	bark	*Rinde*	
	paring	a thin piece that has been cut off the surface	
	stave [steɪv]	long stick, staff	
	lively	here: resilient, springing back to its original form after being bent	
	to whittle into shape	to cut thin strips of wood to give it a certain shape	
	to catch s. o. out	to catch s. o. doing s. th. wrong	
	flagrant [ˈfleɪgrənt]	not hidden in any way, open, shocking	
	to make amends	to compensate for bad things done in the past, to atone	
	to his dismay	with a sudden feeling of fear and alarm	
244	**weal** [wi:l]	mark on the skin caused by a whip, a sword, etc.	*198*

	trickle	a thin, slow stream
	to pull up	to slow down and stop
	to be violently sick	to vomit in a painful way
	to tip	to place at one end
	to nock	to put a v-shaped cut into s. th. (here: for the bowstring)
	raid [reɪd]	sudden surprise attack
245	**armoury** ['ɑːmərɪ]	place where weapons are kept
	compunction	feeling of guilt or regret
	… touched his hat	i. e. as a greeting
	stove-pipe hat	a tall hat like that worn in the 19th century
	wireless	(now old-fashioned) radio
	to scowl [skaʊl]	to frown angrily
	ingratiating	overly friendly in an attempt to gain s. o.'s favour
	profoundly	(form.) very
	coquettish	usually said of women: playful to be attractive to men, flirting
	to uncoil	to unwind 199
	crown	the top part of a hat
	antennae [æn'teniː]	(plural of "antenna") aerials
	peak [piːk]	the front part of a hat, over the eyes
	brim	*Krempe*
	jack-in-the-box	a child's toy: a box with a figure in it, mounted on a spring *(Schachtelmännchen)*
	waspy ['wɒspɪ]	like a wasp
	stethoscopic	as can be heard with a stethoscope
	wheeze	sound like noisy breathing
	crackle ['krækl]	short sharp sounds *(Knistern)*
246	**Primo**	possibly named after Miguel Primo de Rivera (1870-1930) Spanish general and dictator
	Mellon	possibly after Andrew Mellon (1855–1937), American financier and industrialist. He was Secretary of the Treasury from 1921 to 1931 and US ambassador to Great Britain from 1931–1932.
	winning	here: attractive, charming, pleasing
	disconcerting	causing anxiety, surprise, or embarrassment
	literalness	precision, exactness (i. e. keeping exactly to what was asked of him)
	well-covered	well protected by clothing and equipment
	foot-and-mouth-baller	word-play on "footballer" and foot-and-mouth disease, *(Maul- und Klauenseuche)*
	coccyx ['kɒksɪks]	small bone at the end of the backbone *(Steiß)*
	sensation …	1. news which attracts a lot of attention; 2. feeling
	gingerly	carefully and cautiously
	luncheon ['lʌntʃən]	lunch
	undeterred [ʌndɪ'tɜːd]	not discouraged
	cautionary	functioning as a warning
	New York Times	Founded in 1851, the *New York Times* is the most influencial and prestigious newspaper in the USA

	Frankfurt … Continuum [kən'tɪnjʊəm]	obviously the *BNW* successor to the *Frankfurter Zeitung*, founded in 1856, a newspaper with an international reputation until 1933; "Continuum" refers to Einstein's Theory of Relativity	*200*
	The Fordian Science Monitor ['mɒnɪtə]	*BNW* version of *The Christian Science Monitor*, published in Boston since 1908 by the Christian Scientists.	
	The Delta Mirror	*BNW's* version of *The Daily Mirror*, a popular, mass-circulation British paper	
247	**benighted** [bɪ'naɪtɪd]	ignorant	
	delusion	false belief	
	switch	small thin stick	
	importunately [-'----]	in a troublesome and annoying way	
	super-charger	a device (invented in 1922) that increases the amount of air that would normally be drawn into the motor of a car or plane *(Kompressor)*	
	tiresome	annoying, boring	
	to liken to	to compare	
	suitor ['su:tə]	a man who seeks to marry a woman	
	maiden ['meɪdn]	unmarried girl or woman	
	vermin ['vɜ:mɪn]	unpleasant, biting insects *(Ungeziefer)*	
	at a stretch	continuously, without interruption	
	lark	a songbird *(Lerche)*	
	tangible ['tændʒəbl]	real enough to be felt	
248	**hoary** ['hɔ:rɪ]	whitish-grey	
	juniper ['dʒu:nɪpə]	*Wacholder*	
	spike	any sharp-pointed object	*201*
	to haunt [hɔ:nt]	to return repeatedly to the mind	
	stab	here: the feeling of being injured with a sharp pointed instrument	
	to wince [wɪns]	to start slightly because of a sudden pain	
	frenzy	a state of wild excitement or agitation	
	frantically	in an extreme state of emotion	
	infamous ['ɪnfəməs]	having a bad reputation, notorious	
	to flog	to beat harshly with a whip, etc.	
	hide	a hiding-place made to look like part of the environment, normally used by hunters, birdwatchers, etc.	
	Darwin	possibly named after Charles Darwin (1809–1882), English naturalist who formulated the theory of evolution by natural selection; or after Charles Darwin's grandfather, Erasmus Darwin (1731–1802), who was said to have made experiments with the creation of embryos	
	Bonaparte	named after Napoleon Bonaparte (1769–1821), French general and Emperor	
	big-game	large animals that are hunted for sport	
	bole	trunk of a tree	
	belly	stomach, front middle part of the body	
249	**glued to**	(fig.) constantly focused on or aimed at	
	their … objective	i. e. the Savage	

	… clapped on a higher power …	quickly added an additional telescopic lens
	close-up	large-scale photo, as if taken from very close
	slow-motion	method of filming at high speed, which is then shown at a slower speed *(Zeitlupe)*
	raving words	wild and furious words
	amplification	increase in loudness
	lull [lʌl]	short period of calm
	accommodating	willing to help, kind, obliging 202
	to mop [mɒp]	to wipe with a handkerchief
	sperm whale	*Pottwal*
	to release	to allow to be shown publicly
	feely-palace	i. e. cinema (cf. the expression "movie palace" used in the 1920s and 1930s)
	rustic [ˈrʌstɪk]	characteristic of the country
250	**And all our yesterdays … dusty death.**	*Macbeth,* V, v (where Macbeth realizes how desperate the situation is, and hears that his wife has committed suicide)
	… a good kissing carrion …	(Hamlet is pretending to be mad at this point; in some versions of this play: "… a god kissing carrion …".) *Hamlet,* II, ii
	carrion [ˈkærɪən]	dead and rotting flesh
	to plant	to place
	As flies … sport	*King Lear,* IV, i (spoken by the Earl of Gloucester after his eyes had been plucked out; see also page 233/*189* under "… God managing things …".)
	wanton	playful
	… ever-gentle gods	*King Lear* IV, vi
	thy best … nor more.	Shakespeare's *Measure for Measure* III, i (spoken by the Duke of Vienna to Claudio, who is condemned to die. He is saying death is no more than sleep.)
	thou oft provok'st	you often bring about
	grossly [ˈgrəʊslɪ]	very much
	Perchance to dream … For in that sleep … dreams …	*Hamlet,* III, i (Hamlet is considering suicide and sees a similarity between sleep and death, but he wonders what kind of dreams you can have when you are dead.)
	perchance	perhaps
	immensities	huge thoughts 203
	deity [ˈdiːɪtɪ]	God
	locust	an insect that destroys crops over large areas *(Feldheuschrecke)*
	poised	not moving, in a state of stillness
	grass-hopper	*Heuschrecke*
	shantung [ʃænˈtʌŋ]	a heavy silk material
	singlet	a piece of clothing without sleeves for men worn under a shirt or instead of one
251	**petits beurres**	(Fr.) sweet biscuits
	cover	a place giving protection
	posture	position, way of holding the body

	at bay	(of a hunted animal) forced to face the attackers because there is no escape	
	stupor ['stju:pə]	state in which one cannot think properly because of shock or drugs	
	babel ['beɪbl]	confusion of voices	
	tormentor	a person who causes suffering or pain	
	plaintive ['pleɪntɪv]	expressing melancholy, sad	
	almond ['ɑ:mənd]	*Mandel*	
252	**propitiation** [-ˌ--'--]	the act of trying to please s. o. who is angry	*204*
	stunt [stʌnt]	anything unusual or spectacular done for attention	
	reiteration [ri:ˌɪtə'reɪʃn]	repetition	
	unanimity [ˌ--'---]	complete agreement, unity	
253	**to recoil** [rɪ'kɔɪl]	to move back suddenly in fear	
	The second passed.	misprint in some editions for: The seconds …	
	inaudibly	not loud enough to be heard	*205*
	impassioned	with strong emotions	
	Fitchew! ['fɪtʃu:]	here used by Cassio in *Othello,* IV, i in the sense of a woman with a bad reputation; cf. also p. 195/*158* for the use of the word "fitchew" by King Lear	
	to slash [slæʃ]	to strike with a whip	
	to bolt	to move suddenly	
	out of harm's way	away from danger	
	whoop [hu:p]	loud joyful cry	
	convergent	moving towards the same point	
	stampede	a crowd of people or animals rushing in an uncontrolled way	
	Fry, lechery, fry!	said by Theresites in *Troilus and Cressida,* V, ii	
	to fry	here: to burn with strong passion	
	lechery	too much interest in sex	
	to scramble	to struggle with others to get s. th.	
	trough [trɒf]	container from which animals can eat or drink	
	Kill it …	i. e. kill sexual desire	
	impelled	forced, urged, driven	
	ineradicably	in such a way that it cannot be removed	
	turpitude	shameful wickedness	
	stupefied	made unable to think clearly	
	sensuality	sexual pleasure	
	archway ['ɑ:tʃweɪ]	a passage or entrance with an arched roof *(Bogengang)*	*206*

1. Why are John, Bernard, and Helmholtz happy? What are the different kinds of happiness?
2. What kind of life does John want to lead in his hermitage? Why? Explain in particular why he whips himself.
3. What aspects of journalism does Huxley criticize? How is this criticism relevant for today?
4. Why does John kill himself in the end? Is his suicide convincing? What seems to be Huxley's message?
5. Explain the symbolism of the last paragraph of the novel.
6. Is John's death tragic?

7 Foreword *7*

	to repent [-'-]	to express a feeling of having done s. th. bad (usu. in a religious context)
	to make amends	to do s. th. to make the situation better again
	on no account	not for any reason
	to brood	to spend too much time thinking about a problem
	muck [mʌk]	dirt, filth, mud
	analogous [-'---]	similar
	to pore over	to look at s. th., study s. th. very carefully
	its first execution	i. e. the first time it was written or published
	to bequeath	to leave behind when one dies or goes away
	futile ['fju:taɪl]	serving no useful purpose
	considerable	great in number
	merits	good points
	to wallow in	to think about an undesirable situation longer than is reasonable, i. e. “rolling in the muck”, as above
	to leave both well and ill alone	to leave both the faults and the merits as they are (ironic use of the fixed expression “to leave well enough alone”)
8	**Utopia**	from the Greek, meaning “no place”; first used by Thomas More in 1516 as the title of his book describing a perfect society
	lunacy	madness, insanity
	for the sake of	for the purpose of
	fertility cult	tribal practice placing great importance on the production of children *8*
	Penitente	a religious order in New Mexico whose members regularly whipped themselves
	ferocity [fə'rɒsətɪ]	violence, intensity
	to warrant ['wɒrənt]	to make proper or necessary for the circumstances, to justify
	acquaintance with	knowledge of
	to retreat	to move away from
	native	natural (to him), coming from his upbringing
	And so they died miserably ever after	cf. the fairy tale ending: “And they lived happily ever after.”
	much to the reassurance of	removing all anxiety from
	Pyrrhonic [pɪ'rɔ:nɪk]	referring to the ancient Greek philosopher Pyrrho; here: sceptical
	aesthete ['i:sθi:t]	a person who has or claims to have the ability to appreciate beauty and art
	author of the fable	the author of this novel, i. e. Huxley himself
	phenomenon [-'---]	
	to compile	to collect for a book
	anthology	a collection of poems, articles, stories, etc.; the anthology in question is probably *The Perennial Philosophy* (1945)
	eminent	famous, well known

hilarious	usu.: very funny; here: giving cause for joyous laughter
benefactor	a person who does s. th. good for society
Pantheon ['pænθɪən]	in ancient Greece or Rome: a temple for all the gods; here: a monument for the dead
gutted	completely destroyed, burnt out
9 **ossuary** ['ɒsjʊərɪ]	a place where the bones of the dead are kept
sacred ['seɪkrɪd]	holy
SI MONUMENTUM REQUIRIS CIRCUMSPICE	"If you seek [hɪs/theɪr] monument, look around." (inscription in St. Paul's Cathedral referring to its architect, Sir Christopher Wren, 1632–1723)
a third alternative	Huxley did write a novel in 1962 entitled *Island*, in which he describes what he thinks is an ideal society.
the ... horns of a dilemma	expression describing a situation where only two alternatives are possible, and both alternatives are equally unpleasant
Henry Georgian	following the theories of Henry George (1839–1897), American econonmist, journalist, and politician. He felt that the cause of inequality in society lay in the private ownership of land. He suggested introducing a tax on land that would take away the profit from buying and selling land. All other taxes would be abolished.
Kropotkinesque	following the theories of Piotr Alesseyevich Kropotkin (1842–1921), a Russian anarchist. He believed it was possible to have a non-competetive society based upon communes of producers linked to each other by voluntary contracts.
Final End	(phil./theol.) ultimate purpose, reason for existence
unitive	tending to become one *9*
immanent	(phil./theol.) of God: permanently part of the universe
Tao	Chinese word for "path". Taoism is a Chinese religion started in the 3rd century B. C. that held that one should avoid striving and attain one's ideal state of being by mystical contemplation alone.
Logos	Greek word for "word", signifing in Greek philosophy the source of world order and understanding
transcendent	(phil./theol.) opposite of "immanent", i. e. (of God) existing apart from the material universe
Godhead	Divine Being *(Gottheit)*
Brahman ['brɑːmən]	in Hinduism: eternal spirit from which all things originate and and then return to
utilitarianism	an ethical system that takes the ultimate good to be the greatest happiness of the greatest number, and defines the rightness of actions in terms of their contribution to the general

		happiness. Jeremy Bentham (1748–1832) and John Stuart Mill (1806–1873) were its main spokesmen.	
	contingency	any event that may occur	
	devoted to	very much involved with, giving a lot of one's time and energy for s. th.	
	pursuit of sanity	cf. "the pursuit of happiness" in the US Declaration of Independence	
10	**vantage point**	perspective	
	inclined plane	flat surface that extends downwards	
	prognostication	prophecy	
	in the ... interval	in the meantime	
	to invalidate	to show that s. th. is not correct	
	foresight	the ability to see what is likely to happen in the future and make good use of it	
	nuclear fission ['fɪʃn]	splitting the (nucleus of the) atom to produce energy	
	Robert Nichols	(1893–1944) English poet and dramatist. Huxley is referring to his play *Wings Over Europe.*	
	to disintegrate	to break up, to split into many pieces	
	nuclei ['nju:klɪaɪ]	pl. of "nucleus"	
	oversight	careless mistake	
	tacitly ['tæsɪtlɪ]	without being openly expressed	
	to take for granted	to assume the existence of	*10*
11	**to modify**	to change a little	
	searching	here: thorough *(gründlich)*	
	Marquis de Sade (1740–1814)	French writer who was often imprisoned for pornography. He saw a connection between sexual pleasure and violence. From him comes the term "sadism."	
	to rationalize	to think of reasonable explanations for non-rational behaviour	
	peculiar	special	
	(Isidore Maximilian de) Robespierre	(1758–1794) a leading figure of the French Revolution who was in part responsible for the Reign of Terror. He was himself executed.	
	superficial	not very deep *(oberflächlich)*	
	(François) Babeuf	(1760–1797) French radical whose views were much like communism. He was executed during the Revolution.	
	apostle [ə'pɒsl]	a person who supports a certain viewpoint	
	henceforward	from that time on	
	to purge	to get rid of, remove completely	
	decencies	normal moral standards	
	laboriously	done with a great deal of effort	
	inhibition	tendency to suppress certain impulses *(Hemmung)*	
	inevitable	unavoidable	
	lunatic	madman	
	penultimate [-'---]	next to the last	
12	**warfare**	fighting a war	
	Thirty Years War	(1618–1648) general European war fought mainly in Germany	*11*

	military resources	weapons, soldiers
	to annihilate [ə'naɪəleɪt]	to destroy, wipe out
	a going concern	a successful enterprise
	fifth Marquess of Lansdowne	Henry Charles Keith Petty Fitzmaurice (1845–1927) British statesman. His letter, however, was accepted and published in the *Daily Telegraph* in 1917.
	famine ['fæmɪn]	a time when there is no food and people starve
	Hiroshima	An atomic bomb was dropped on the Japanese city of Hiroshima on August 6, 1945.
	Magdeburg	In 1631, during the Thirty Years War, Tilly and Pappenheim stormed the city and killed the defending troops. A fire destroyed most of the city.
	to harness	here: to bring s.th. under control and use it
13	**to disrupt**	to break up, to bring into disorder
	Procrustes [prəʊ'krʌsti:z]	in Greek mythology, a robber who forced passers-by to lie on a bed and then stretched them to fit it or sawed off their legs if they were too long
	applied science	science used in a practical way
	to get into one's stride	to start to do s.th. with confidence at a faster pace *(in Schwung kommen)*
	predominantly	mainly, for the most part *12*
	statism ['steɪtɪzəm]	the concentration of all political and economic power in the state
	club	heavy stick
	by … firing squads	i.e. by shooting people
	inhumane	cruel
	demonstrably	easily shown or proven
	sin against the Holy Ghost	(ironic) the worst sin of all
	executive [-'---]	the authority that makes decisions and sees that they are carried out
14	**to coerce** [kəʊ'ɜ:s]	to force
	servitude	condition of being a slave
	to assign to	to give to
	crude	not completely worked out, rough, not refined
	Jesuits ['dʒezjʊɪts]	members of a Roman Catholic order known as the Society of Jesus. It has a reputation for strict discipline and a tradition of learning and science.
	to boast	to talk about s.th. one is proud of
	to answer for	to take responsibility for
	pedagogue ['pedəgɒg]	(form., slightly derog.) teacher
	reverend	term of respect given to a priest
	reverend fathers	i.e. the Jesuits who educated him
	Voltaire	(1694–1778), French philosopher and writer who supported religious and political liberty. For his attacks against the establishment he was often imprisoned. His ideas had a great influence on the French Revolution.

	to refrain from	to not do s. th. one would like to	
	(Winston) Churchill	(1874–1965), British statesman and prime minister (1940–1945, 1951–1955). He created the expression "iron curtain" in a speech he gave in 1946 warning about Soviet expansion in Europe.	
	denunciation	extreme criticism in public of s. th. believed to be wrong or evil	
	compelling	convincing, persuasive	
	rebuttal	proving s. th. to be wrong *(Widerlegung)*	
	liquidation	systematic killing	*13*
	friction	conflict	
	Manhattan Project	code name for the US Army project established in 1942 to develop the atomic bomb as quickly as possible. It involved many eminent scientists.	
	inquiry	investigation	
	for the sake of brevity ['brevətɪ]	i. e., in order to keep this foreword short	
15	**scopolamine** [skə'pɒləˌmiːn]	$C_{17}H_{21}NO_4$, a drug used as a sedative (with morphine) or as a "truth serum"	
	discontent	not being satisfied, condition of being unhappy or dissatisfied	
	narcotic	a drug that reduces pain or causes sleepiness	
	at once	here: at the same time	
	foolproof	so well designed that nothing can go wrong	
	eugenics [juː'dʒenɪks]	the study of methods of improving the quality of the human race	
	to facilitate	to make easier	
	semimoron	a person who is rather stupid	
	feature	characteristic	
	soma	a drug in *BNW* used to make people happy	
	hypnopaedia	learning of lessons heard during sleep	
	caste [ɑː]	a certain social class	
	promiscuity [ˌ--ɪ---]	having many different sexual partners	*14*
16	**licence**	an official document showing that one has the permission to do s. th.	
	cannon fodder	food for cannons, i. e. soldiers who might have to die in a war	
	he … will do well to	it is advisable for him to	
	in conjunction with	together with	
	dope	drugs	
	to project	here: to place (in a particular time)	
	may be upon us	may happen	
	smithereens [ˌsmɪðə'riːnz]	little pieces	
	end	*Zweck*	
	means	*Mittel*	
	root	basic cause	
	perpetuation	continuation of s. th. for a long time	
	supra-national	above all national interests	
	You pays your money … choice.	ironic phrase first used in *Punch* magazine in 1846	

1. What main fault did Huxley (in 1946) find in his own novel? Do you agree that it would have been better to give the Savage "a third alternative"(p.9/*8*)? What alternative might there be?
2. If Huxley were alive to write a new Foreword today, do you think he would find different "failure [s] of foresight" (p.10/*9*)? (Consider both technological and social developments.)

Material for Further Study

Some Important Utopias and Dystopias

1. The Garden of Eden, *Genesis* Chs. 2 and 3: The recurrent idea of a golden era in the distant past – here given a theological dimension: the temptation of the devil and man's downfall.
2. *The Republic*, Plato (Greek philosopher, 429-347 B.C.): The prototype of a totalitarian state with a stratified society of warriors and workers ruled by philosophers; shared goods, sexual equality, controlled breeding, only healthy children permitted to live, communal child care, censorship of the arts.
3. *City of God*, Saint Augustine (354-430 A.D.): He believed man to be basically depraved and saw sexuality as s.th. sinful except for the purposes of procreation – saw all of human history as God's plan – true Christians would achieve immortality in the mystical City of God; he has had a profound influence on Christian theology, influencing such theologians as Calvin and Jansen.
4. *Utopia* (1516), Sir Thomas More (leading English humanist, 1478-1535): The first to use the expression "utopia". His was a community ruled by reason alone: no private property, free clothing and meals, education for all, all religions tolerated. Many of More's contemporaries believed a utopia could be achieved in the New World.
5. *Émile* (1762), Jean-Jacques Rousseau (major French philospher and educator, 1712-1778): He believed there was a golden past before man became distanced from nature, and developed the idea of the "noble savage" uncorrupted by civilization. The end of *Émile* gives a summary of Rousseau's idea of a social order: he was distrustful of a pure democracy and proposed that a class of "shepherds" should ensure that the general will was kept intact.
6. *Looking Backward* (1888), Edward Bellamy (American writer, 1850-1898): His novel was a best-seller in its time. His utopia depicted a socialist system set in Boston. There is no material want and people work not for material gain but for honour and prestige.
7. *Erewhon* (1872), Samuel Butler (1835-1902): His novel anticipates the satiric utopias of Huxley and Orwell. He is very critical of the belief in eternal progress. In the society of the Erewhonians, machines have been destroyed as dangerous competitors and disease is considered a crime worthy of punishment.

8. *A Modern Utopia* (1905), H.G. Wells (1866-1946): He thought of a utopia with a world state, with state contol of land, capital and industry and population; there would be voluntary rulers called Samurai. He continued his ideas in *Men Like Gods* (1925).
9. *We* (1925), Yevgeny Zamyatin (Russian writer, 1884-1937): This novel anticipates the plots of *Brave New World* and *1984* – the hero unsuccessfully challenges a state where workers have numbers rather than names, eat chemical food, are controlled in their sexual activity, and are ruled by a Benefactor, who is always re-elected.
10. *Brave New World* (1932), Aldous Huxley (1894-1963): The classic satire of a scientific utopia, in many ways a satire of English and American society after World War One.
11. *1984* (1949), George Orwell (1903-1950): A totalitarian state that uses terror to suppress its citizens: historical records are destroyed, language is controlled ("Newspeak"), there is no love or privacy, sex is very much frowned upon except for the purposes of procreation, the eternal Big Brother rules. As in *We* and *Brave New World*, a rebellious hero unsuccessfully tries to challenge the state.
12. *Walden Two* (1948), B.F. Skinner (American psychologist, 1904-1990): An ideal society organized according to behaviourist principles.
13. *Fahrenheit 451* (1954), Ray Bradbury (American writer, b. 1920): A totalitarian society in which books of all kinds are forbidden.
14. *Island* (1962), Aldous Huxley: Huxley's last novel, describing an ideal state which incorporates some aspects of *Brave New World* society, e.g. communal life with loose "voluntary family" units, liberal sexuality, eugenics, use of mind-expanding drugs, an educational system that uses hypnosis and conditioning; there is a strong influence of Eastern mystical religions.

dystopia imaginary place where everything is bad (cf. page 97: Thomas More's pun "eutopia" = good place) – 1 **Genesis** ['dʒenəsɪs]first book of the Old Testament – **recurrent** happening repeatedly – 2 **stratified** with distinct groups arranged with one above the other – 3 **Augustine** [ɔː'gʌstɪn] – **depraved** morally bad, corrupt – **procreation** producing children – 4 **contemporaries** people who lived at the same time – 6 **to depict** to describe – 7 **to anticipate** to do s.th. in advance – 8 **Samurai** ['sæmʊraɪ] the class of warriors in feudal Japan – 9 **benefactor** ['--,--] usu.: person who supports schools, hospitals, etc. with help or money – 11 **to frown upon** to disapprove of – 14 **to incorporate** to include – **eugenics** [juː'dʒenɪks] the science of improving the human race

Background Ideas

1. On Utopias

This summary is by the well-known behaviourist psychologist, B. F. Skinner, himself the author of a "Utopia".

A collection of cultural designs is to be found in the utopian literature. Writers have described their versions of the good life and suggested ways of achieving them. Plato, in *The Republic*, chose a political solution;

Saint Augustine, in *The City of God*, a religious one. Thomas More and Francis Bacon, both lawyers, turned to law and order, and the Rousseauean utopists of the eighteenth century, to a supposed natural goodness in man. The nineteenth century looked for economic solutions, and the twentieth century saw the rise of what may be called behavioral utopias in which a full range of social contingencies began to be discussed (often satirically).

Utopian writers have been at pains to simplify their assignment. A utopian community is usually composed of a relatively small number of people living together in one place and in stable contact with each other. They can practice an informal ethical control and minimize the role of organized agencies. They can learn from each other rather than from the specialists called teachers. They can be kept from behaving badly toward each other through censure rather than the specialized punishments of a legal system. They can produce and exchange goods without specifying values in terms of money. They can help those who have become ill, infirm, disturbed, or aged with a minimum of institutional care. Troublesome contacts with other cultures are avoided through geographical isolation (utopias tend to be located on islands or surrounded by high mountains), and the transition to a new culture is facilitated by some formalized break with the past, such as a ritual of rebirth (utopias are often set in the distant future so that the necessary evolution of the culture seems plausible). A utopia is a total social environment, and all its parts work together. The home does not conflict with the school or the street, religion does not conflict with government, and so on.

Perhaps the most important feature of the utopian design, however, is that the survival of a community can be made important to its members. The small size, the isolation, the internal coherence – all these give a community an identity which makes its success or failure conspicuous. The fundamental question in all utopias is conspicuous. The fundamental question in all utopias is "Would it really work?" The literature is worth considering just because it emphasizes experimentation. A traditional culture has been examined and found wanting, and a new version has been set up to be tested and redesigned as circumstances dictate. […]

It is not surprising that, so far as the real world is concerned, the word utopian means unworkable. History seems to offer support; various utopian designs have been proposed for nearly twenty-five hundred years, and most attempts to set them up have been ignominious failures. But historical evidence is always against the probability of anything new; that is what is meant by history. Scientific discoveries and inventions are improbable; that is what is meant by discovery and invention. And if planned economies, benevolent dictatorships, perfectionistic societies, and other utopian ventures have failed, we must remember that unplanned, undictated, and unperfected cultures have failed too. A failure is not always a mistake; it may simply be the best one can do under the circumstances. The real mistake is to stop trying. Perhaps we cannot now design a successful culture as a whole, but we can design better practices in a piecemeal fashion. The behavioral processes in the world at large are the same as those in a utopian community, and practices have the same effects for the same reasons.

From *Beyond Freedom and Dignity* by B.F. Skinner, New York: Knopf 1972, pp. 153-156.

5 **Francis Bacon** (1561-1626) English philosopher and statesman who believed that experiments were the only way to arrive at scientific truth. He proposed a scientific utopia in his book *The New Atlantis*. – 6 **Rousseauean** like Jean-Jacques Rousseau (1718-1778) – 8 **behavioral** guided by the principles of behavioural psychology, which sees all behaviour in terms of stimulus and response – 9 **contingency** possible arrangement – 11 **to be at pains to do s.th.** to do s.th. with a great deal of effort – **assignment** [əˈsaɪnmənt] task – 17 **censure** [ˈsenʃə] strong disapproval or criticism – 19 **infirm** weak because of poor health – 20 **disturbed** here: with mental problems – 31 **coherence** [kəʊˈhɪərəns] quality of fitting together logically – 32 **conspicuous** [kənˈspɪkjʊəs] obvious, easily noticed – 37 **to dictate** here: to make necessary – 41 **ignominious** [ˌɪgnəˈmɪnɪəs] shameful, disgraceful – 47 **undictated** not ruled by a single authority – 51 **in a piecemeal fashion** by degrees, bit by bit

The ancients called me Utopia or Nowhere because of my isolation. At present, however, I am a rival of Plato's republic, perhaps even a victor over it. The reason is that what he has delineated in words I alone have exhibited in men and resources and laws of surpassing excellence. Deservedly ought I to be called by the name of Eutopia or Happy Land.

From the introduction to More's *Utopia*, 1516, translated from the Latin by G.C. Richards, 1923. The "map of the island of Utopia" is a woodcut from the original edition.

ancients those from the far past – 11 **to delineate** to describe, to portray – 15 **surpassing** exceptional, extraordinary

2. A Scientific Revolution

Huxley's grandfather, a distinguished scientist, is the author of this view of 19th century developments.

The most obvious and the most distinctive features of the History of Civilisation, during the last fifty years, is the wonderful increase of industrial production by the application of machinery, the improvement of old technical processes and the invention of new ones, accompanied by an even more remarkable development of old and new means of locomotion and intercommunication. By this rapid and vast multiplication of the commodities and conveniences of existence, the general standard of comfort has been raised; the ravages of pestilence and famine have been checked; and the natural obstacles, which time and space offer to mutual intercourse, have been reduced in a manner, and to an extent, unknown to former ages. The diminution or removal of local ignorance and prejudice, the creation of common interests among the most widely separated peoples, and the strengthening of the forces of the organisation of the commonwealth against those of political or social anarchy, thus effected, have exerted an influence on the present and future fortunes of mankind the full significance of which may be divined, but cannot, as yet, be estimated at its full value.

This revolution – for it is nothing less – in the political and social aspects of modern civilisation has been preceded, accompanied, and in great measure caused, by a less obvious, but no less marvellous, increase of natural knowledge, and especially of that part of it which is known as Physical Science, in consequence of the application of scientific method to the investigation of the phenomena of the material world.

From *The Advance of Science in the Last Half-Century* by T. H. Huxley, New York 1887, pp. 203-5.

6 **locomotion** the ability to move from place to place – 7 **commodity** [kəˈmɒdətɪ] anything of use – **convenience** any device that is labour-saving – 8 **ravages** [ˈrævɪdʒɪz] (usu. pl.) destructive action – 10 **intercourse** communication or exchange – 11 **diminuation** decrease – 14 **commonwealth** here: a community organized for the common good – 16 **to divine** to guess – 22 **in consequence of** as a result of

3. The Factory at Night

When soothing darkness spreads
O'er hill and vale,
And when the punctual stars,
While all things else are gathering to their homes,
Advance, and in the firmament of heaven
Glitter – but undisturbing, undisturbed;
As if their silent company were charged
With peaceful admonitions for the heart
Of all-beholding Man, earth's thoughtful lord;

Then, in full many a region, that once was
The assured domain of calm simplicity
And pensive quiet, an unnatural light
Prepared for never-resting Labour's eyes,
Breaks from a many-windowed fabric huge;
And at the appointed hour a bell is heard,
Of harsher import than the curfew knell
That spoke the Norman Conqueror's stern behest:
A local summons to unceasing toil!
Disgorged are now the ministers of day;
And, as they issue from the illumined pile,
A fresh band meets them, at the crowded door
And in the courts, and where the rumbling stream
That turns the multitude of dizzy wheels
Glares, like a troubled spirit, in its bed
Among the rocks below. Men, maidens, youths,
Mothers and little children, boys and girls
Enter, and each the wonted task resumes
Within this temple, where is offered up
To Gain, the master idol of the realm,
Perpetual sacrifice.

Poem by William Wordsworth (1770-1850).

1 **soothing** calming, making quiet and peaceful – 2 **o'er** (lit.) over – **vale** (lit.) valley – 8 **admonition** warning – 12 **pensive** thoughtful – 14 **fabric** factory – 16 **import** here: meaning, importance – **curfew knell** the ringing of the evening bell – 17 **behest** (poet.) command – 18 **summons** call, invitation, admonition – 19 **to disgorge** to throw out as from the throat – **minister of day** here: day worker – 20 **illumined** illuminated – **pile** here: factory building – 22 **to rumble** to move along making a dull, vibrating sound, e.g. like distant thunder – 23 **dizzy** here: causing dizziness, i.e. a confused feeling in the head as if everything were turning round – 27 **wonted** [əʊ] customary, habitual – 29 **realm** [ə] kingdom, country

4. The Grand Inquisitor

One of the characters in Dostoevsky's novel The Brothers Karamazov *writes a "prose poem" in which an official of the Spanish Inquisition speaks to Jesus Christ. Here is part of what he says.*

"Was it not you who said so often in those days, "I shall make you free"? But now you have seen those "free" men. Yes, this business has cost us a great deal, but we've completed it at last in your name. For fifteen centuries we've been troubled by this freedom, but now it's over and done with for good. You don't believe that it is all over? You look meekly at me and do not deign even to be indignant with me? I want you to know that now – yes, today – these men are more than ever convinced that they are absolutely free, and yet they themselves have brought their freedom to us and humbly laid it at our feet. But it was we who did it. And was that what you wanted? Was that the kind of freedom you wanted? [. . .]

There has been no lack of warnings and signs, but you did not heed the warnings. You rejected the only way by which men might be made happy, but, fortunately, in departing, you handed on the work to us. [. . .] We have corrected your great work and have based it on *miracle, mystery, and authority.* And men rejoiced that they were once more led like sheep and that the terrible gift which had brought them so much suffering had at last been lifted from their hearts. Were we right in doing and teaching this? Tell me. Did we not love mankind when we admitted so humbly its impotence and lovingly lightened its burden and allowed men's weak nature even to sin, so long as it was with our permission? Why, then, have you come to meddle with us now? And why are you looking at me silently and so penetratingly with your gentle eyes? [. . .]

Oh, this work is only beginning, but it has begun. We shall have to wait a long time for its completion and the earth will have yet much to suffer, but we shall reach our goal and be Caesars and it is then that we shall think about the universal happiness of man. [. . .] Yes, we shall force them to work, but in their leisure hours we shall make their life like a children's game, with children's songs, in chorus, and with innocent dances. [. . .] And they will all be happy, all the millions of creatures, except the hundred thousand who rule over them. For we alone, we who guard the mystery, we alone shall be unhappy.

There will be thousands of millions of happy infants and one hundred thousand sufferers who have taken upon themselves the curse of knowledge of good and evil."

From *The Brothers Karamazov* (1880) by Fyodor Dostoevsky, translated by David Magarshack, London 1958; pp. 294-304 Penguin edition.

6 **meekly** obediently, timidly, without any pride – **to deign** [deɪn] to do s.th. even though you think you are too important to do such a thing – **indignant** shocked and angry – 12 **to heed** to take notice of – 16 **to rejoice** to feel or show great joy – 20 **impotence** ['ɪmpətəns] inability to take strong action – 22 **to meddle** to interfere without being asked – 34**curse** [kɜːs] s.th. that causes great harm or destruction (*Fluch*)

5. Life in a Scientific Society

Philosopher Bertrand Russell belonged to Huxley's social circle. In his book The Scientific Outlook *he regards a society based on scientific principles as a real possibility.*

The advantages to be derived from an organized World State are great and obvious. There will be, in the first place, security against war and a saving of almost the whole effort and expense now devoted to competitive armaments. [. . .].

There will, of course, be a universal language, which will be either Esperanto or pidgin-English. The literature of the past will for the most part not be translated into this language, since its outlook and emotional background will be considered unsettling: serious students of history will be able to obtain a permit from the Government to study such works as *Hamlet* and *Othello*, but the general public will be forbidden access to them on the ground that they glorify private murder; boys will not be allowed to read books about pirates or Red Indians; love themes will be discouraged on the ground that love, being anarchic, is silly, if not wicked. All this will make life very pleasant for the virtuous. [...]

Education in a scientific society may, I think, be best conceived after the analogy of the education provided by the Jesuits. The Jesuits provided one sort of education for the boys who were to become ordinary men of the world, and another for those who were to become members of the Society of Jesus. In like manner, the scientific rulers will provide one kind of education for ordinary men and women, and another for those who are to become holders of scientific power. Ordinary men and women will be expected to be docile, industrious, punctual, thoughtless, and contented. Of these qualities probably contentment will be considered the most important. In order to produce it, all the researches of psycho-analysis, behaviourism, and biochemistry will be brought into play. [...]

Science, when it has once acquired a firm hold upon social organization, is hardly likely to stop short at those biological aspects of human life which have hitherto been left to the joint guidance of religion and instinct. We may, I think, assume that both the quantity and the quality of the population will be carefully regulated by the State, but that sexual intercourse apart from children will be regarded as a private matter so long as it is not allowed to interfere with work.

If we were right in supposing that the scientific society will have different social grades according to the kind of work to be performed, we may assume also that it will have uses for human beings who are not of the highest grade of intelligence. It is probable that there will be certain kinds of labour mainly performed by negroes, and that manual workers in general will be bred for patience and muscle rather than for brains. The governors and experts, on the contrary, will be bred chiefly for their intellectual powers and their strength of character.

From *The Scientific Outlook* by Bertrand Russell. London: George Allan & Unwin Ltd. 1931, pp. 219-221, 251-253, 259-262.

4 **armaments** (usu. pl.) weapons for war – 6 **pidgin-English** a simplified version of English that is mixed with another language – 7 **outlook** general attitude, perspective – 8 **unsettling** causing disatisfaction or worry – 10 **access** the right to use s.th. – 14 **virtuous** here: behaving correctly according to the moral code of a society – 15 **to conceive** to imagine – 16 **Jesuit** ['dʒezjʊɪt] a member of the Society of Jesus, a Roman Catholic religious order founded in 1534 – 22 **docile** ['dəʊsaɪl] obedient, easily controlled – 23 **thoughtless** here: unable to think – 29 **hitherto** up to now – 32 **apart from children** when not producing children – 35 **grade** here: class – 39 **to breed (bred, bred)** *züchten*

6. The Power to Begin the World All Over Again

Why did the conviction of the corruptibility of men and the vulnerability of states – and the consequent idea of America as experiment – give way to the delusion of a sacred mission and a sanctified destiny? The original conviction was rooted in realistic conceptions of history and of human nature – conceptions that waned as the republic prospered. The intense historical-mindedness of the Founding Fathers did not endure. Though the first generation came to Philadelphia loaded down with historical examples and memories, its function was precisely to liberate its progeny from history. Once the Founders had done their work, history commenced on a new foundation and in American terms. "We have it in our power," Tom Paine said in *Common Sense*, "to begin the world all over again." Emerson defined himself as the endless seeker, with no Past at his back. "The Past," Melville said in *White-Jacket*, "is dead, and has no resurrection; but the Future is endowed with such a life, that it lives to us even in anticipation."

The process of narcissistic withdrawal from history, much commented on by foreign travelers, was sustained by the simultaneous withdrawal, after 1815, from the power embroilments of the old world. The new nation was largely populated by people torn from, fleeing from, or in revolt against their own histories. This also helped take the republic out of the movement and motive of secular history. "Probably no other civilised nation," said the *Democratic Review* in 1842, "has ... so completely thrown off its allegiance to the past as the American." But the nineteenth century was steeped in history compared to the twentieth. Today, for all the preservation of landmarks and the show biz of bicentennials, we have become, so far as interest and knowledge are concerned, an essentially historyless people. Businessmen agree with the elder Henry Ford that history is bunk. The young no longer study history. Academics turn their backs on history in the enthusiasm for the ahistorical behavioral "sciences." As the American historical consciousness has thinned out, the messianic hope has flowed into the vacuum.

From *The Cycles of American History* by Arthur M. Schlesinger, Jr. London: André Deutsch 1987, pp. 16-17.

1 **vulnerability** [ˌvʌlnərəˈbɪlətɪ] being open to attack or damage – 3 **sanctified** here: approved of by God, holy, sacred – 5 **to wane** to lessen, to become weaker – 6 **Founding Fathers** the Americans who helped to write the US Constitution in Philadelphia in 1787 – **to endure** to last – 8 **progeny** [ˈprɒdʒənɪ]descendants – 11 **Tom Paine** [peɪn](1737-1809) British-born radical politician and writer. His pamphlet *Common Sense* (1776) contained the demand that the 13 American colonies immediately declare their independence from Great Britain. – 12 **Emerson** Ralph Waldo Emerson (1803-1882), American writer and philosopher – 13 **Melville** [ˈmelvɪl]Herman Melville (1819-1891), a major American writer. *White Jacket* (1850) is a novel about life on the sea. – 14 **to endow with s. th.** [enˈdaʊ]to provide with certain qualities – **... lives to us ... in anticipation** ... seems to be real for us before it happens – 16 **narcissistic** [ˌnɑːsɪˈsɪstɪk]thinking very much of oneself, admiring oneself very much – 17 **to sustain** to continue, to maintain, to keep up – 18 **1815** 1815 marked the end of the second conflict with Great Britain. For the next 100 years the USA seldom involved itself in the affairs of Europe. – **embroilment** conflict – 21 **secular** here: having to do with political developments among states –

22 *Democratic Review* a monthly political journal published between 1837 and 1849 – 24 **to be steeped in s.th.** to be very much influenced by s.th. – 25 **show biz** (sl.) show business, the entertainment industry – 26 **bicentennial** [ˌbaɪsenˈtenɪəl]the celebration of s.th. that happened 200 years ago – 29 **academic** a student or teacher at a university – 30 **ahistorical** [ˌeɪhɪsˈtɒrɪkəl]not concerned with history – **behavioral "sciences"** e.g. psychology, sociology – 31 **messianic** having to do with the idea that one has a mission to guide and improve the world

The Making of *Brave New World*

7. American Diary

Aldous Huxley visited the United States in 1926, and published his impressions in book form. Here is an extract.

Mother's Day. But why not Flapper's Day? It would be more representative, more democratic, so to speak. For in Joy City there are many more Flappers – married as well as unmarried – than Mothers.

Thousands and thousands of flappers, and almost all incredibly pretty. Plumply ravishing, they give, as T.S. Eliot has phrased it, a "promise of pneumatic bliss.' Of pneumatic bliss, but of not much else, to judge by their faces. So curiously uniform, unindividual and blank. Hardly more expressive – to the foreign eye, at any rate – than any of the other parts of that well-contoured anatomy which they are at such pains to display. [. . .]

We climbed into our host's car and drove, it seemed interminably, through the immense and sprawling city. Past movie palaces and theatres and dance halls. Past shining shops and apartments and enormous hotels. On every building the vertical lines of light went up like rockets into the dark sky. And the buildings themselves – they too had almost rocketed into existence. Thirty years ago Los Angeles was a one-horse – a half-horse – town. In 1940 or thereabouts it is scheduled to be as big as Paris. As big and as gay. The great Joy City of the West.

And what joy! The joy of rushing about, of always being busy, of having no time to think, of being too rich to doubt. The joy of shouting and bantering, of dancing and for ever dancing to the noise of the savage music, of lustily singing.

Yes, sir, she's my Baby.
No, sir, don't say "Maybe."
Yes, sir, she's my Baby now.

The joy of loudly laughing and talking at the top of the voice about nothing. (For thought is barred in this City of Dreadful Joy and conversation is unknown.) The joy of drinking prohibited whiskey from enormous silver flasks, the joy of cuddling provocatively bold and pretty flappers, the joy of painting the cheeks, of rolling the eye and showing off the desirable calves and figure. The joy of going to the movies and the theatre, of sitting with one's fellows in luxurious and unexclusive clubs, of trooping out on summer evenings with fifty thousand others to listen to concerts in the open air, of being always in a crowd, never alone. The joy of going on Sundays to hear a peppy sermon, of melting at the hymns, of repenting one's sins, of getting a kick out of uplift. The joy, in a word, of having what is technically known as a Good Time.

From *Jesting Pilate* by Aldous Huxley, London 1926;
pp. 191-193 Triad edition, 1985.

1 **flapper** a young woman who in the 1920s rejected the conventions of society, wore short skirts, etc. – 5 **plump** well-rounded and full in form – **ravishing** ['ræv--] attractive, delightful, lovely – **T.S. Eliot** (1888-1965) American-born writer and poet who settled in England – 7 **blank** showing no expression, empty of thought – 9 **well-contoured** ['kɒntʊərd] well-shaped – **to be at pains to do s.th.** to make a great effort to do s.th. – 11 **interminable** [ɪn'tɜːmɪnəbl] endless – 12 **sprawling** ['sprɔːlɪŋ] spread out in many different directions – **movie palace** an especially large and luxurious cinema – 21 **to banter** ['bæntə] to talk in a teasing or joking manner – 22 **lusty** full of joy and energy – 23 **Yes, sir she's my Baby...** a popular song of the 1920s – 27 **to bar** to exclude, to prohibit, to ban – 28 **prohibited whiskey** From 1919 to 1932 alcoholic drinks were not allowed to be sold in the USA. – 29 **flask** a small flat bottle – **to cuddle** ['kʌdl] to hold a person close to show affection – 31 **calf** (**pl. calves**) *Wade* – 33 **to troop out** to walk outside in a group – 35 **peppy** lively – **sermon** *Predigt* – 36 **to repent one's sins** to feel sorry about what one has done wrong – **to get a kick out of s.th.** (sl.) to get a strong feeling of pleasure or excitement from doing s.th. – **uplift** ['ʌplɪft] here: the religious message and atmosphere that makes one feel better

8. Entertainment for the Masses

That increased leisure does not lead to increased culture among the leisured is due to two main causes, one hereditary and the other environmental. A great many men and women – let us frankly admit it, in spite of all our humanitarian and democratic prejudices – do not want to be cultured, are not interested in the higher life. For these people existence on the lower, animal levels is perfectly satisfactory. Given food, drink, the company of their fellows, sexual enjoyment, and plenty of noisy distractions from without, they are happy. They enjoy bodily, but hate mental, exercise. They cannot bear to be alone, or to think. Contemporary urban life, with its jazz bands, its negroid dancing, its movies, theaters, football matches, newspapers, and the like, is for them ideal. They can live out their lives without once being solitary, without once making a serious mental effort (for the work which most of these people do is mainly mechanical and requires little or no thought), without once being out of sight or sound of some ready-made distraction. The notion that one can derive pleasure from arduous intellectual occupations is to such people merely absurd. More leisure and more prosperity mean for them more dancing, more parties, more movies, more distractions in general. Most of the inhabitants of ancient Rome belonged to this type; so probably do most of the inhabitants of modern New York and London. And unless some system of eugenics is practiced in the interval, there is no reason to suppose that the inhabitants of the great cities in the year 3000 A.D. will be radically different. Machines are giving universal leisure, and universal leisure makes universal culture a possibility. But a large proportion of human beings are so constituted that they do not want to actualize that possibility. [...]

The machines give leisure; but at the same time they give what is almost a guarantee that, except by a fortunately situated and well-endowed minority, that leisure shall be misused. Machinery creates prosperity and leisure by enabling men to manufacture enormous numbers of exactly similar objects in a short time. Mass production is an admirable thing when applied to material objects; but applied to the things of the spirit it is not so good. It might be good if the spiritual wares retailed by our mass-producers of the mind were of high quality. But they are not. As things are at present, mass-produced material objects are of much better quality than mass-produced ideas and mass-produced art. The material standard is higher. A boot factory whose finished products were as thoroughly shoddy as the products of the average idea- or art-factory would go bankrupt in a few months. Everybody objects to leaky ill-fitting boots; but only a small minority objects with anything like the same intensity to imbecile ideas and vulgarity in art.

From "The Outlook For American Culture" by Aldous Huxley, in *Harpers Magazine*, August 1927, p. 26.

8 **distraction** anything that amuses or entertains – **from without** from outside of oneself – 10 **negroid** ['ni:grɔɪd] typical of the negro race – 12 **solitary** single, alone – 16 **arduous** requiring great mental or physical effort – 21 **eugenics** [ju:dʒenɪks]the science of improving the human race – 22 **in the interval** in the meantime – 26 **to be constituted** to be formed or made up – **to actualize** to realize, to make use of – 29 **fortunately situated** in a good social position, belonging to the upper classes – **well-endowed** rich, with a high income – 35 **to retail** ['ri:teɪl]to sell to the consumer – 39 **shoddy** of poor quality – 40 **leaky** allowing water to get in – 42 **imbecile** ['ɪmbəsi:l] extremely stupid

9. Interview with Aldous Huxley

INTERVIEWERS: Would you tell us something first about the way you work?
HUXLEY: I work regularly. I always work in the mornings, and then again a little bit before dinner. I'm not one of those who work at night. I prefer to read at night. I usually work four of five hours a day. I keep at it as long as I can, until I feel myself going stale. Sometimes, when I bog down, I start reading – fiction or psychology or history, it doesn't much matter what – not to borrow ideas or materials, but simply to get started again. Almost anything will do the trick.
INTERVIEWERS: Do you do much rewriting?
HUXLEY: Generally, I write everything many times over. All my thoughts are second thoughts. And I correct each page a great deal, or rewrite it several times as I go along. [...]

INTERVIEWERS: Do you block out chapters or plan the over-all structure when you start out on a novel?

HUXLEY: No, I work away a chapter at a time, finding my way as I go. I know very dimly when I start what's going to happen. I just have a very general idea, and then the thing develops as I write. Sometimes – it's happened to me more than once – I will write a great deal, then find it just doesn't work, and have to throw the whole thing away. I like to have a chapter finished before I begin on the next one. But I'm never entirely certain what's going to happen in the next chapter until I've worked it out. Things come to me in driblets, and when the driblets come I have to work hard to make them into something coherent.

I've always considered myself very lucky to be able to make a living at something I enjoy doing. So few people can.

INTERVIEWERS: Do you ever use maps or charts or diagrams to guide you in your writing?

HUXLEY: No, I don't use anything of that sort, though I do read up a good deal on my subject. Geography books can be a great help in keeping things straight. I had no trouble finding my way around the English part of *Brave New World*, but I had to do an enormous amount of reading up on New Mexico, because I'd never been there. I read all sorts of Smithsonian reports on the place and then did the best I could to imagine it. I didn't actually go there until six years later, in 1937, when we visited Frieda Lawrence.

INTERVIEWERS: When you start out on a novel, what sort of a general idea do you have? How did you begin *Brave New World*, for example?

HUXLEY: Well, that started out as a parody of H. G. Wells' *Men Like Gods*, but gradually it got out of hand and turned into something quite different from what I'd originally intended. As I became more and more interested in the subject, I wandered farther and farther from my original purpose.

INTERVIEWERS: What are you working on now?

HUXLEY: At the moment I'm writing a rather peculiar kind of fiction. It's a kind of fantasy, a kind of reverse *Brave New World*, about a society in which real efforts are made to realize human potentialities. I want to show how humanity can make the best of both Eastern and Western worlds. So the setting is an imaginary island between Ceylon and Sumatra, at a meeting place of Indian and Chinese influence. One of my principal characters is, like Darwin and my grandfather, a young scientist on one of those scientific expeditions the British Admiralty sent out in the 1840s; he's a Scotch doctor, who rather resembles James Esdaile, the man who introduced hypnosis into medicine. And then, as in *News from Nowhere* and other utopias, I have another intruder from the outside world, whose guided tour provides a means of describing the society. Unfortunately, he's also the serpent in the garden, looking enviously at this happy, prosperous state. I haven't worked out the ending yet, but I'm afraid it must end with paradise lost – if one is to be realistic. [...]

INTERVIEWERS: How did you happen to start writing? Do you remember?

HUXLEY: I started writing when I was seventeen, during a period when I was almost totally blind and could hardly do anything else. I typed out a novel by the touch system; I couldn't even read it. I've no idea what's become of it; I'd be curious to see it now, but it's lost. My aunt, Mrs. Humphry Ward, was a kind of literary godmother to me. I used to have long talks with her about writing; she gave me no end of sound advice. She was a very sound writer herself. [...] Then later, during the war and after, I met a great many writers through Lady Ottoline Morrell. She used to invite all kinds of people out to her country house. I met Katherine Mansfield there, and Siegfried Sassoon, and Robert Graves, and all the Bloomsburies. I owe a great debt of gratitude to Roger Fry. Listening to his talk about the arts was a liberal education. At Oxford I began writing verse. I had several volumes of verse published before I turned to writing stories. I was very lucky; I never had any difficulty getting published. After the war, when I came down from Oxford, I had to make my living. I had a job on the *Athenaeum*, but that paid very little, not enough to live on; so in spare moments I worked for the Condé Nast publications. I worked for *Vogue* and *Vanity Fair*, and for *House and Garden*. I used to turn out articles on everything from decorative plaster to Persian rugs. And that wasn't all. I did dramatic criticism for the *Westminster Review*. Why – would you believe it? – I even did music criticism. I heartily recommend this sort of journalism as an apprenticeship. It forces you to write on everything under the sun, it develops your facility, it teaches you to master your material quickly, and it makes you look at things. Fortunately, though, I didn't have to keep at it very long. [...]

INTERVIEWERS: To return to writing, in *Point Counter Point* you have Philip Quarles say, "I am not a congenital novelist." Would you say the same of yourself?

HUXLEY: I don't think of myself as a congenital novelist – no. For example, I have great difficulty in inventing plots. Some people are born with an amazing gift for storytelling; it's a gift which I've never had at all. One reads, for example, Stevenson's accounts of how all the plots for his stories were provided in dreams by his subconscious mind (what he calls the "Brownies" working for him), and that all he had to do was to work up the material they had provided. I've never had any Brownies. The great difficulty for me has always been creating situations.

INTERVIEWERS: Developing character has been easier for you than creating plots?

HUXLEY: Yes, but even then I'm not very good at creating people; I don't have a very wide repertory of characters. These are difficult things for me. I suppose it's largely a question of temperament. I don't happen to have the right kind of temperament.

INTERVIEWERS: By the phrase "congenital novelist" we thought you meant one who is only interested in writing novels.

HUXLEY: I suppose this is another way of saying the same thing. The congenital novelist doesn't have other interests. Fiction for him is an absorbing thing which fills up his mind and takes all his time and energy, whereas someone else with a different kind of mind has these other, extracurricular activities going on.

From *Writers at Work: The Paris Review Interviews, Second Series*, New York: The Viking Press 1963, pp. 197-206.

6 **to go stale** (fig.) to lose energy or ideas because of overwork – **to bog down** (fig. coll.) to become stuck and unable to go on – 14 **to block out**

to make an outline of s.th. – 17 **dimly** vaguely – 23 **driblet** a small amount – 24 **coherent** [ˌkəʊ'hɪərənt] logical, orderly, making sense – 34 **Smithsonian** produced by the Smithsonian Institution in Washington D.C., a museum that concerns itself, among other things, with the study of the American Indian – 36 **Frieda Lawrence** the wife of D.H. Lawrence (who died in 1930). She lived at that time in Taos, New Mexico. – 39 **H.G. Wells** (1866-1946) English writer on politics, history and society. His novel *Men Like Gods* (1925) was about a utopia in which everyone lives in harmony. (cf. page 95.) – 45 **... peculiar kind of fiction..** i.e. *Island* published in 1962 – 47 **potentiality** unused power or possibility – 49 **Ceylon** [sɪ:lɒn] an island to the southeast of India now called Sri Lanka – 50 **Sumatra** an island that is part of Indonesia – 51 **Darwin** Charles Darwin (1809-1882) English naturalist who formulated the theory of evolution by natural selection – **my grandfather** i.e. Thomas Huxley (1825-1895), who supported Darwin's views (cf. text 2) – 52 **Admiralty** ['ædmərəltɪ] the government department in charge of the navy – 54 *News From Nowhere* Utopian novel written by William Morris in 1890. – 55 **intruder** a person who enters a place without permission – 57 **serpent** snake (reference to the Garden of Eden) – 59 **paradise lost** an allusion to Milton's epic poem of the same name (1667) – 66 **Mrs. Humphry Ward** (1851-1920) English novelist – 68 **no end of** a lot of – **sound** reasonable, sensible, showing good judgement – 70 **Lady Ottoline Morrell** (1873-1938) a wealthy woman who often entertained and supported well-known writers. – 72 **Katherine Mansfield** (1888-1923) writer of short stories, born in New Zealand – **Siegfried Sassoon** (1886-1967) English poet – **Robert Graves** (1895-1985) English poet and novelist – 73 **Bloomsburies** i.e. writers, artists and intellectuals who lived and worked in and around Bloomsbury, London. They were known as the Bloomsbury Group. **Roger Fry** [fraɪ] (1866-1934) English art critic and painter – 74 **liberal** here: helping to develop cultural and intellectual interests – 77 **...came down from..** left Oxford University after graduation – 78 *Athenaeum* [ˌæθɪ'nɪ:əm](1828-1931) a weekly literary review – 79 **Condé Nast** a British publisher – 80 *Vogue* a fashion magazine – *Vanity Fair* (1914-1936) magazine that reviewed literature, art and fashion – *House and Garden* magazine that gives the latest trends in furniture and interior decorating – 83 *Westminster Review* a literary and cultural magazine – 84 **heartily** very much – 85 **apprenticeship** the time when one learns a skill, time of training – 86 **facility** skill – 89 *Point Counter Point* novel written in 1928 (cf. introduction, page 3) – 90 **congenital** [kən'dʒenɪtl] as if from birth – 95 **Stevenson** Robert Louis Stevenson (1850-1894), Scottish writer – 110 **absorbing** taking all one's attention – 112 **extracurricular** [ˌekstrəkə'rɪkjʊlə] here: other than work (usu.: outside the school curriculum)

10. What is Huxley Worrying About? (A book review)

Brave New World, by Aldous Huxley. New York: Doubleday, Doran and Company. $2.50.
With war in Asia, bankruptcy in Europe and starvation everywhere, what do you suppose Aldous Huxley is now worrying about? If you happen to

have read an article he published about a year ago in The Virginia Quarterly Review, you will be able to guess. He is worrying about the unpleasantness of life in the utopia that, as he sees it, is just a century or two ahead.

"Brave New World" is, as one would expect, a somewhat amusing book; a bright man can do a good deal with two or three simple ideas. Mr. Huxley assumes that, six hundred years from now, mass-production methods have been perfected, Freudian psychology has triumphed, and certain biological experiments, notably in the field of ectogenesis, have borne fruit. The result is a world in which reproduction is left to the laboratories and sex is made a game. People are rigorously divided into classes, and the members of each class are prepared in the test-tube and conditioned in childhood for the kind of life their class leads. Everybody is encouraged to consume as much as possible everybody is made to believe he is happy, and prevented from doing any thinking on his own account.

For the sake of dramatic interest, Mr. Huxley introduces three rebels, two of them members of the ruling class, one restless because of physical shortcomings, the other because of intellectual superiority. The former brings to England the third rebel, who has been brought up in a New Mexican reservation for the segregation of unassimilated peoples. It is the savage, of course, who most vigorously resents the monotony and emptiness of life in the year 632 After Ford, and who most violently insists on the individual's right to suffer in order to develop his soul. [...] It is difficult to suppose that Mr. Huxley is really much concerned about God and romance and the beauty of motherhood, but he sees that there is something to be said for them, and the whole argument does show that after all human nature is human nature. [...]

This is a pretty horrid picture Mr. Huxley paints, and he can be sure that any of us, after reading his book, will think twice before taking steps that might bring about such a calamity. Perhaps we had better not do anything about social injustice or international anarchy. A quotation in the front of "Brave New World" points out that utopias are almost inevitable and that a day will come when intellectuals will dream of ways of avoiding utopias and returning to a society less "perfect" but freer. The better way, the book shows, is here and now to nip the utopias in the bud. After all, Mr. Huxley must have his chance to suffer and be brave.

Apparently we have been doing Mr. Huxley an injustice in thinking of him as a bored, cynical and generally rebellious young man. He is, on the contrary, quite well satisfied with life as it is. And why, when you stop to think of it, shouldn't he be? He has money, social position, talent, friends, prestige, and he is effectively insulated from the misery of the masses. Of course he demands the right to suffer bravely. Of course he wants something to worry about – even if he has to go a long, long way to find it.

Review by Granville Hicks in *The New Republic*, New York, 1932.

1 ... **War in Asia...** a reference to the Japanese invasion of Manchuria (in China) in 1931 – **bankruptcy in Europe** a reference to the Great Depression of the 1930s, the worst economic crisis of the 20th century that indirectly led to World War Two – 11 **ectogenesis** the growth of an

organism outside the body it would normally be found in, e.g. the growth of an embryo outside the mother's body – 12 **to bear** (bore, borne) **fruit** [beə/bɔː/bɔːn] to have a successful result – 21 **shortcoming** defect, fault, failing – 33 **calamity** disaster, misfortune – 38 **to nip in the bud** to stop s. th. before it can properly develop (*etwas im Keim ersticken*) – 40 **to do s. o. an injustice** to misjudge s. o. – 44 **insulated** [ˈɪnsjʊleɪtɪd] protected and separated

Brave New World Revisited

11. A Tract Against Materialism

It is a well-understood convention that the Utopian kind of pseudo-novel, though set in a remote position as to period or place, is always a criticism of the author's own society. *Brave New World* is a criticism of Western society in 1932, as *1984* is of the same society in the closing months of the Second World War; any discussion of such books that sets out to assess their plausibility as *predictions* seems to me hopeless off-centre. The citizens of the Brave New World are entirely conditioned to a life which ignores the possibility of any values except those of pleasure and material well-being; they live in great physical comfort which is paid for in terms of an appalling spiritual dryness. As a criticism of the more prosperous Western countries in the late "twenties' it could not be bettered; the "prophetic" framework is valuable largely because it allows free play to the author's marvellous wit (the jokes about Ford, etc.).

The thrust against materialism had point in 1932, and has point now; but in the actual future, I doubt if it will have any. People who live very primitive and physically exhausting lives are never materialistic; on the contrary, they are always deeply religious. And it will, of course, be a primitive and laborious life that human beings will live in a hundred years' time and indefinitely thereafter; even if there are no World Wars, the increase of population, coupled with the exhaustion of natural resources, will usher in an era of famine and shortage. Our great-grandchildren will listen open-mouthed to stories of the 1950's, when even quite ordinary people had motor cars of their own, to go more or less where they liked, and could buy petrol without a police permit; people who lived in houses which could be warmed by merely switching on an electric fire, and where hot water gushed out of the taps! I think, in short, that humanity has already reached the most highly urbanized and gadget-ridden state it is ever likely to reach; anyone who wants to know how the peoples of the Western countries will be living in a century's time could find out more from a tour of South-East Asia than anything else: that swarming, half-starved proletariat – *that* is our future, not a world in which ordinary citizens take trips by helicopter from London to New York.

It was the brave *old* world that Mr. Huxley was describing; the world with a tremendous material ascendancy, whose natural danger was sceptical materialism. In the world we are actually going to inhabit, the dangers will be devil-worship and witch-burning. But this fact does not, of course, diminish the value of Mr. Huxley's works.

From the article "Tracts Against Materialism: *After Many a Summer* and *Brave New World*" by John Wain in *The London Magazine*, 1955; reprinted in *Aldous Huxley: A Collection of Critical Essays*, ed. Robert E. Kuehn, New York: Prentice Hall 1974, pp. 28-29.

tract essay – 1 **convention** a generally accepted opinion – 5 **to set out to do s.th.** to start trying to do s.th. – 6 **to assess** [-ˈ-]to evaluate, to determine, to estimate – **off-centre** far from being correct – 10 **appalling** [əˈpɔːlɪŋ] shocking, terrible – 14 **thrust** here: attack – **point** purpose, value – 18 **laborious** needing much work – 21 **to usher in** to mark the beginning of s.th. – 26 **to gush** to pour out suddenly and in great amounts – 28 **gadget-ridden** dominated by a great number of small machines – 31 **swarming** present in large numbers – 35 **ascendancy** position of greatest achievement – 37 **witch** *Hexe*

12. From Huxley's *Brave New World Revisited*, 1958

a) *A comparison with* Nineteen Eighty-Four:
George Orwell's *Nineteen Eighty-Four* was a magnified projection into the future of a present that contained Stalinism and an immediate past that had witnessed the flowering of Nazism. *Brave New World* was written before the rise of Hitler to supreme power in Germany and when the Russian tyrant had not yet got into his stride. In 1931 systematic terrorism was not the obsessive contemporary fact which it had become in 1948, and the future dictatorship of my imaginary world was a good deal less brutal than the future dictatorship so brilliantly portrayed by Orwell. In the context of 1948, *Nineteen Eighty-Four* seemed dreadfully convincing. But tyrants, after all, are mortal and circumstances change. Recent developments in Russia and recent advances in science and technology have robbed Orwell's book of some of its gruesome verisimilitude. A nuclear war, will, of course, make nonsense of everybody's predictions. But, assuming for the moment that the Great Powers can somehow refrain from destroying us, we can say that it now looks as though the odds were more in favour of something like *Brave New World* than of something like *Nineteen Eighty-Four.*

3 **to witness** to see; here: to be the setting or scene of s.th. – **flowering** the full development – 4 **rise of Hitler** Hitler was appointed chancellor of Germany at the end of January 1933. *Brave New World* was first published in 1932. – 5 **Russian tyrant** i.e. Joseph Stalin – **to get into one's stride** here: (fig.) to make full use of one's political power (Huxley is alluding to Stalin's liquidation of the opposition 1934-1937.) – 6 **obsessive** being constantly thought of – **contemporary** existing at a certain time, current – 8 **to portray** to describe, to present a picture of – 11 **recent developments** After Stalin's death in 1953 there was a lessening of tension between the West (USA and Europe) and the Soviet Union. In the late 50s the Soviet leader Krushchev (1953-1964) introduced a number of reforms that increased the personal freedom of Soviet citizens. – 12 **gruesome** horrible, frightful – 13 **verisimilitude** [ˌverɪsɪˈmɪlɪtjuːd] appearance of being true – 14 **Great Powers** i.e. the USA and the Soviet Union – 15 **to refrain from doing s.th.** to keep oneself from doing s.th. – 16 **the odds** the probability

b) On entertainment:

In the past most people never got a chance of fully satisfying this appetite. They might long for distractions, but the distractions were not provided. Christmas came but once a year, feasts were “solemn and rare’, there were few readers and very little to read, and the nearest approach to a neighbourhood movie theatre was the parish church, where the performances, though frequent, were somewhat monotonous. For conditions even remotely comparable to those now prevailing we must return to imperial Rome, where the populace was kept in good humour by frequent, gratuitous doses of many kinds of entertainment – from poetical dramas to gladiatorial fights, from recitations of Virgil to all-out boxing, from concerts to military reviews and public executions. But even in Rome there was nothing like the non-stop distraction now provided by newspapers and magazines, by radio, television and the cinema. In *Brave New World* non-stop distractions of the most fascinating nature (the feelies, orgy-porgy, centrifugal bumblepuppy) are deliberately used as instruments of policy, for the purpose of preventing people from paying too much attention to the realities of the social and political situation. The other world of religion is different from the other world of entertainment; but they still resemble one another in being most decidedly “not of this world’. Both are distractions and, if lived in too continuously, both can become, in Marx’s phrase, “the opium of the people’ and so a threat to freedom.

1 **this appetite** i.e. the need for entertainment – 2 **distraction** anything that amuses or entertains – 5 **approach** here: similarity – 7 **remotely** in the slightest way – **prevailing** predominant, widespread – 8 **imperial Rome** the Roman Empire, from 31 B.C. to 180 A.D. at the height of its power – **populace** ['pɒpjʊləs] the masses – 9 **gratuitous** [grət'tju:ɪtəs] done without payment expected – **dose** *Dosierung* – 10 **gladiatorial** with men trained to fight in arenas for entertainment – **recitation** reading of poetry before an audience – **Virgil** ['vɜ:dʒɪl] (70 B.C. – 19 B.C.) one of the greatest Roman poets – 11 **all-out** complete, in its pure form, with no restrictions – **review** a formal parade of soldiers in the presence of a king, president, etc. – 20 **“not of this world’** cf. John 8:23 where Jesus says “I am not of this world.” – 21 **Marx** Karl Marx (1818-1883), founder of communism; the phrase “Religion... is the opium of the people.” is from his *Critique of Hegel’s Philosophy of Right*.

c) On brainwashing:

Brainwashing, as it is now practised, is a hybrid technique, depending for its effectiveness partly on the systematic use of violence, partly on skilful psychological manipulation. It represents the tradition of *1984* on its way to becoming the tradition of *Brave New World*. Under a long-established and well-regulated dictatorship our current methods of semi-violent manipulation will seem, no doubt, absurdly crude. Conditioned from earliest infancy (and perhaps also biologically predestined) the average middle- or lower-caste individual will never require conversion or even a refresher course in the true faith. The members of the highest caste will have to be able to think new thoughts in response to new situations: consequently their training will be much less rigid than the training imposed upon those whose business is not to reason why, but merely to do and die with the minimum of fuss. These upper-caste individuals will be members, still, of a wild species – the trainers and guardians, themselves only slightly conditioned, of a vast herd of completely domesticated animals. Their wildness will make it possible for them to become heretical and rebellious. When this happens they will have to be either liquidated, or brainwashed back into orthodoxy, or (as in *Brave New World*) exiled to some island, where they can give no further trouble, except of course to one another. But universal infant conditioning and the other techniques of manipulation and control are still a few generations away in the future. On the road to the Brave New World our rulers will have to rely on the transitional and provisional techniques of brainwashing.

1 **hybrid** ['haɪbrɪd] of mixed origin – 6 **crude** not done carefully, not completely worked out – 8 **caste** [kɑ:st] very rigid social class – **conversion** change in which a person accepts a completely new religion or belief – 9 **refresher course** a course of instruction to bring one up-to-date with the latest developments or techniques – **the true faith** i.e. the principles of the state – 12 **business** here: purpose in life – **...not to reason why...** cf. "Their's not to reason why, Their's but to do and die..." from "The Charge of the Light Brigade" by Alfred Lord Tennyson (English poet, 1809-1892) – 13 **fuss** [fʌs] too much bother or concern – 14 **species** ['spi:ʃi:z] here: a particular group of individuals who have the same characteristics – 15 **guardian** someone who looks after the welfare of others – 17 **heretical** maintaining beliefs that do not conform with the beliefs of the established authoritites – 18 **to liquidate** to kill – 23 **transitional** for a period of time until changes can be made –

d) On birth control:

How can we control the vast impersonal forces that now menace our hard-won freedoms? On the verbal level and in general terms, the question may be answered with the utmost ease. Consider the problem of overpopulation. Rapidly mounting human numbers are pressing ever more heavily on natural resources. What is to be done? Obviously we must, with all possible speed, reduce the birth rate to the point where it does not exceed the death rate. At the same time we must, with all possible speed, increase food production, we must institute and implement a world-wide policy for conserving our soils and our forests, we must develop practical substitutes, preferably less dangerous and less rapidly exhaustible than uranium, for our present fuels; and, while husbanding our dwindling resources of easily available minerals, we must work out new and not too costly methods for extracting these minerals from ever poorer and poorer ores – the poorest ore of all being sea water. But all this, needless to say, is almost infinitely easier said than done. The annual increase of numbers should be reduced. But how? We are given two choices – famine, pestilence and war on the one hand, birth control on the other. Most of us choose birth control – and immediately find ourselves confronted by a problem that is simultaneously a puzzle in physiology, pharmacology, sociology, psychology and even theology. "The Pill' has not yet been perfected. When and if it is perfected, how can it be distributed to the many hundreds of millions of potential mothers (or, if it is a pill that works upon the male, potential fathers) who will have to take it if the birth-rate of the species is to be reduced? And, given existing social customs and the forces of cultural and psychological inertia, how can those who ought to take the pill, but don't want to, be persuaded to change their minds? And what about the objections on the part of the Roman Catholic Church to any form of birth control except the so-called Rhythm Method – a method incidentally, which has proved, hitherto, to be almost completely ineffective in reducing the birth-rate of those industrially backward societies where such a reduction is most urgently necessary? And these questions about the hypothetically perfect Pill must be asked, with as little prospect of eliciting satisfactory answers, about the chemical and mechanical methods of birth control already available.

From *Brave New World Revisited* by Aldous Huxley, London 1958, pp.204-5, 60-63, 108-109, 179-180.

1 **to menace** ['menəs] to threaten – 3 **utmost** greatest – 4 **mounting** increasing – 8 **to institute** to organize, to establish – 9 **to implement** to put into action – 11 **exhaustible** easily used up, consumed – 12 **to husband** to use economically – **to dwindle** to become gradually less until nothing remains – 14 **ore** *Erz* – 21 **"the Pill"** An oral contraceptive was put on the market in the late 1960s. It is now no longer popular because of its side effects. – 24 **..."the male"** A contraceptive for males by means of an injection has since been developed, but has not seen widespread use. – 25 **species** here: the human race – 26 **inertia** [ɪ'nɜːʃə]resistance to change – 30 **Rhythm Method** having sex only when the woman is least likely to conceive. This method of birth control is the only method approved of by the Roman Catholic Church. – **incidentally** *übrigens* – **hitherto** until now – 34 **to elicit** to bring out, to call forth

13. Second Thoughts (A book review)

This critic refers back to his 1932 review of Huxley's novel. (See text 10.)

Aldous Huxley, who in his early years seemed a lively immoralist, has spent the past two decades and more in preaching. He is preaching again in **"Brave New World Revisited"** (Harper, $3), and I confess that I look back wistfully to the novels he wrote in the Twenties – "Chrome Yellow" and "Antic Hay" and "Point Counter Point." On the other hand, I am willing to listen to this particular sermon, for it is concerned with matters of importance. "Brave New World," it is appropriate to note, marked the transition from the flippant or the apparently flippant Huxley to the serious Huxley.

When I read the book in the year of its publication, it made me angry, not because of Huxley's new seriousness but because of what he had chosen to be serious about. In 1932, when our economic system was falling apart, Huxley was writing about the dangers of utopia and the importance of the right to suffer. As I looked about me, I could see no dearth of suffering, and utopia had never seemed further off. Huxley's thesis, I felt, could please only the reactionary minority, those who did not care how much the majority suffered so long as they could preserve their privileges.

I have reread "Brave New World," and my 1932 judgment seems right for 1932. I do, however, perceive virtues in the book that in 1932 I minimized or overlooked. It has a great deal of comic inventiveness and an ingeniously constructed story, and these qualities make it more readable than most of the books published in 1932. Furthermore, I am compelled to admit that Huxley saw things that I didn't see; in certain respects he was a bit of a prophet.

Obviously we in 1958 are a long way from the situation Huxley envisaged. We are still confronted with the dangers of war, which he doesn't discuss – "not as being unimportant but merely for convenience and because I have discussed them on earlier occasions." And we have an ever more urgent problem of overpopulation, which he does discuss with great cogency. ("Penicillin, DDT, and clean water are cheap commodities, whose effects on public health are out of all proportion to their cost.") We are far from the stability that is requisite for the kind of society portrayed in "Brave New World."

Still and all, there are some significant resemblances between life in A.F. 632 and life in prosperous postwar America, and these are what Huxley makes the most of in "Brave New World Revisited."

Review by Granville Hicks in the *Saturday Review*, New York, November 15, 1958, p. 12.

4 **wistfully** full of sadness, vaguely longing for s. th. that can longer be obtained – 8 **flippant** not showing enough seriousness, disrespectiful – 12 **...economic system...apart...** The author is alluding to the economic crisis in the 1930s known as the Great Depression. – 15 **dearth** [dɜ:θ] lack, scarcity – 27 **to envisage** [ɪn'vɪzɪdʒ] to foresee – 31 **cogency** ['kəʊdʒənsɪ] quality of being convincing – **DDT** a substance used to kill insects (later banned for its adverse effects on animals and humans) – 32 **commodity** an article of trade or commerce – 33 **requisite** ['rekwɪzɪt] necessary

14. Was Huxley Right?

Neil Postman claims that in consuming present-day TV culture we are in effect "amusing ourselves to death." His book, which caused a sensation when it appeared in 1985, relates such developments to Huxley's prophecies.

We were keeping our eye on 1984. When the year came and the prophecy didn't, thoughtful Americans sang softly in praise of themselves. The roots of liberal democracy had held. Wherever else the terror had happened, we, at least, had not been visited by Orwellian nightmares.

But we had forgotten that alongside Orwell's dark vision, there was another – slightly older, slightly less well known, equally chilling: Aldous Huxley's *Brave New World*. Contrary to common belief even among the educated, Huxley and Orwell did not prophesy the same thing. Orwell warns that we will be overcome by an externally imposed oppression.

But in Huxley's vision, no Big Brother is required to deprive people of their autonomy, maturity and history. As he saw it, people will come to love their oppression, to adore the technologies that undo their capacities to think.

What Orwell feared were those who would ban books. What Huxley feared was that there would be no reason to ban a book, for there would be no one who wanted to read one. Orwell feared those who would deprive us of information. Huxley feared those who would give us so much that we would be reduced to passivity and egoism. Orwell feared that the truth would be concealed from us. Huxley feared the truth would be drowned in a sea of irrelevance. Orwell feared we would become a captive culture. Huxley feared we would become a trivial culture, preoccupied with some equivalent of the feelies, the orgy porgy, and the centrifugal bumblepuppy. As Huxley remarked in *Brave New World Revisited*, the civil libertarians and rationalists who are ever on the alert to oppose tyranny "failed to take into account man's almost infinite appetite for distractions." In *1984*, Huxley added, people are controlled by inflicting pain. In *Brave New World*, they are controlled by inflicting pleasure. In short, Orwell feared that what we hate will ruin us. Huxley feared that what we love will ruin us.

From *Amusing Ourselves to Death* by Neil Postman, London: William Heinemann Ltd. 1985, pp. vii-viii (Foreword).

1 **1984** also the title of Orwell's novel – 6 **chilling** frightening – 24 **civil libertarian** a person who is concerned about basic rights such as freedom of speech and religion – **ever on the alert** always watchful and prepared – 26 **distraction** anything that entertains or amuses – 27 **to inflict** to cause a pain, injury, etc. to be suffered

Annotations for text 15, page 117:
pressing demanding immediate attention, urgent – 1 **within the bounds of** possible for – 2 **ruddy** ['rʌdɪ] pink and healthy-looking – 10 **petri dish** ['pi:trɪ] a small dish with a cover used in laboratories to grow bacteria, etc. – 11 **womb** [wu:m] the organ in a woman's body where the embryo grows – 13 **to commission** to give s.o. the job of doing s.th. – 17 **veil** [veɪl] *Schleier* (here fig.) – 22 **clinical researcher** a person who does research in a hospital with patients – 23 **procreation** reproduction, producing children – 24 **to outstrip** to go farther than – 27 **test-tube** *Retorte* – 30 **dawning** beginning – 31 **ominously** ['ɒmɪnəslɪ] causing fear of what might happen – 32 **bleak** [bli:k] dismal, gloomy – 37 *in vitro* [ˌɪn'vi:trəʊ] (Lat.) by artificial means outside the body of a woman – 38 **conception** (from v. **to conceive**) the union of the male and female sex cell – **positively** very much, extremely – **quaint** [kweɪnt] attractive because of being old-fashioned – 42 **artificial insemination** *künstliche Befruchtung* – 45 **venture** a course of action with risks – 54**contraception** *Empfängnisverhütung* – 58 **proposition** matter, task, problem – 63 **dubious** ['dju:bɪəs]doubtful – 65 **retarded** slow in mental or physical development – 67 **offspring** child – 81 **across the board** in all cases – 83 **stricture** ['strɪktʃə] severe criticism – 89 **audacious** [ɔ:'deɪʃəs] bold, daring – 90 **eugenic** [ju:'dʒenɪk] concerned with improving the quality of the human race – 91 **contemporary** current, occurring at the present time

15. Making High-Tech Babies

Science's brave new world raises pressing medical, legal and ethical questions.

It is quite within the bounds of medical science today to create a squealing, ruddy-faced, utterly normal human baby with no fewer than five recognizable parents. One would be the woman who actually bears the child, its mother in the conventional sense. Two others, its "genetic" parents, would supply the sperm and egg that doctors—and perhaps they should count, too—mix in a petri dish and then implant as a living embryo in the "surrogate" mother's womb. Finally come the infant's "real" parents: an otherwise infertile couple who commissioned the whole project and will take the baby home and call it theirs.

That hypothetical child—who may already have been born, behind a veil of secrecy to protect its privacy—personifies the revolution that is now under way in the making of human life. With a speed that amazes some observers and alarms others, doctors and clinical researchers around the globe are achieving powers over procreation that far outstrip traditional law and conventional morality.

It was almost seven years ago that the world's first "test tube" baby, "Louise Brown," was born in a British hospital. At the time, public reaction mixed sheer wonder with vague concerns about the dawning of an ominously engineered human future—the bleak vision of Aldous Huxley's 1932 novel "Brave New World." But by comparison with the techniques available today—donated sperm and eggs, frozen embryos, even the first hints of genetic manipulation—little Louise Brown's simple *in vitro* conception looks positively quaint. More than a thousand test-tube babies are alive today. As many as a quarter of a million children worldwide owe their existence to artificial insemination, which used sperm from men other than their legal fathers. What were once highly experimental ventures have become virtually routine. And as the range of possibilities expands, the whole field of "artificial" or "alternative" birth has suddenly found itself confronted by pressing medical, legal and ethical questions that would have been simply hypothetical a decade ago.

Open Ended: In purely philosophical terms, the issues parallel longstanding debates over abortion and contraception, most significantly on the basic question of what constitutes life and when it begins. But by its very nature, the making of human life is an open-ended proposition, and science today is pushing its doors wide indeed. Is a child conceived in a petri dish different from one made in a marriage bed? Should surrogate motherhood, widely viewed as ethically dubious if not illegal, be allowed in certain circumstances? But suppose the child is born deformed or retarded? Does a man who donates sperm have any obligations—or rights—to the eventual offspring? Do all married couples—or homosexuals, or single people—have a "right to reproduce," by whatever means? Is there any reason to invest millions of dollars to create babies artificially in an overcrowded world? Should governments regulate the new techniques—and if so, how? And should limits be put on the increasingly controversial field of embryo research?

Whatever the answers to those perplexing and potentially explosive questions, the use of high-tech baby-making is virtually certain to grow. The Roman Catholic Church opposes it virtually across the board: no procreation without sex has been added to the older stricture against sex without procreation. Nevertheless, there is a clear demand for the new techniques among millions of frustrated, would-be parents, who by some estimates number as many as one married couple in seven. Even at its most audacious—including proposals for eugenic experiments to eliminate inherited diseases—contemporary reproductive science remains far from the infant assembly-line vision of "Brave New World." But the foundations for something perhaps uncomfortably like it are already clearly in place, and fundamental decisions will have to be made on how to control it.

From *Newsweek*, New York, March 18, 1985, pp. 42-43.

16. Furor Makes Book a Hit

YUKON – The most popular book at Yukon High School is Aldous L. Huxley's 1932 classic "Brave New World."

"Every copy in the library has been checked out," said Yukon superintendent Darrell Hill.

The reason for the sudden readers' demand for the book is that it has been removed from classroom study in the advanced English classes, while the Yukon school board investigates a written complaint against the book.

The stepfather of one student has complained the book contains sexual innuendos and is "futuristic and humanistic," Hill said.

Hill said the board has an established procedure for dealing with written complaints about books.

The board appoints a committee of seven people to read the book, review it together and write a report, which is then submitted to the board.

Hill said the committee is composed of two parents – one of whom is the complaining person – two principals, two teachers and one central office employee.

Hill expects the report to be submitted to the board within the next few days.

If the complaining person or the board does not agree with the report, it can be appealed, Hill said. If an agreement cannot be reached administratively, the matter can be taken to court, he said.

The superintendent said when the complaint was registered the man had asked only that his stepchild not read the book.

Hill said the student was offered a choice of about 100 other books to read.

Then the stepfather decided he wanted the book removed from the school entirely so as not to "change the values" of other students reading it.

Hill described the students in the advanced English class as 17- and 18-year olds, with IQs of 125 to 150.

Ironically, the World Book encyclopedia notes that Huxley wrote "Brave New World" as a protest because he believed science was destroying human and political values.

Article by Ellie Sutter in *The Daily Oklahoman*, May 6, 1988.

furor public protest – 1 **Yukon** ['ju:kɒn] a small town in Oklahoma, USA – 8 **superintendent** a person who oversees schools – 16 **board** an official group with a special responsibility – 22 **innuendo** a remark that suggests s.th. negative without being direct – 24 **humanistic** here derog.: concerned only with human matters, and rejecting God – 35 **to submit** to present for judgement, to hand in – 40 **principal** ['prɪnsəpl] head of a school – 49 **to appeal** to formally ask a higher authority to change a decision made by a lower authority – 73 **World Book encyclopedia** an encyclopedia published in the USA for high school students

17. The On-Going Critical Discussion

a) *On the possibility of a scientific utopia:*

1. It may well be that only biologists and philosphers will really appreciate the full force of Mr Huxley's remarkable book. For of course in the world at large, those persons, and there will be many,

who do not approve of his "utopia", will say, we can't believe all this, the biology is all wrong, it couldn't happen. Unfortunately, what gives the biologist a sardonic smile as he reads it, is the fact that the *biology is perfectly right.* *Joseph Needham, 1934*

2. It is interesting to speculate on the possibilities of a test-tube revolution. One faulty product could distort the entire human race and the future of the world simply by tampering with the test tubes. *Jenni Calder, 1976*

3. As we have seen in Germany and Russia, freedom in scientific research is incompatible with dictatorship. [..] Scientific dictatorships will perish through not being sufficiently scientific. *Bertrand Russell, 1952*

4. *Brave New World* may profitably be compared with the late George Orwell's *1984*, which, allowing for the fact that it was written nearly twenty years later, seems a far more plausible (and even more depressing) vision of the future than Mr. Huxley's. *Jocelyn Brooke, 1954*

5. Utopia is a bad word today not because we despair of being able to achieve it but because we fear it. Utopia itself [...] has become the enemy. *Robert Elliot, 1970*

b) *On Huxley's attitude to his "utopia":*

1. A life-span without war, violence and the dread of cruel disease – is it not worth the silly slogans, the scent organ, the Feelies and the lack of an unknown freedom? But the [...] price is deep and graduated human relationships, is virtue, is courage, endurance, faith exchanged for uniformity and spiritual squalor. There is no doubt on which side Aldous comes down on. *Sybille Bedford, 1973*

2. Reading Huxley today, it is the author rather than the inhabitants of his brave new world that seems naive. Like Mustapha Mond [...] many of us now shudder about the dangerous intimacies of family life, with its mother brooding over her children like a talking cat. *Elaine Baruch, 1979*

3. The absence of suffering in Mustapha Mond's utopia is attributable to the systematic eradication of precisely those attributes of human nature that Huxley himself found most objectionable. It is this fact that accounts for the curiously ambiguous quality of Huxley's social criticism in *Brave New World*. [...] A significant number of Mustapha Mond's principal beliefs, including his repudiation of history, disavowal of the value of the individual ego, dismissal of unlimited historicist progress, rejection of art, and aversion for the family, were shared at this time by Huxley. *Robert S. Baker, 1982*

c) *On the characters:*

1. Bernard Marx and Helmholtz Watson could not have been enlarged into full-scale antagonists of their society without violating the conception of the novel [...]. John is needed, then.
Rudolf B. Schmerl, 1962

2. Lenina's is hardly a "grand passion" in the vein of a Juliet; and the Savage, with his prudish fear of sex and hypocritical disdain for Lenina's frank sexuality, is a poor Romeo. But the very suggestion of a development in Lenina, following the impulse to pursue her happiness, is an indication that the stuff of a very different sort of happiness – and the possibility of tragedy – is a potentiality of even so debased a culture as Brave New World. *Krishan Kumar, 1987*

3. Most obviously, the Savage exercises self-restraint; he realizes that without restraint there is lust but never love; hence his apparently absurd behavior toward Lenina. When he fails to restrain himself, as in the orgy at the end of the novel, he ceases to be "civilized" (on his own terms), and therefore kills himself. *Peter Firchow, 1984*

4. It is finally the agonizing longing to be alone that drives the Savage to suicide. *John Hawley Roberts, 1937*

5. The Savage's suicide cannot be attributed solely to the pernicious impact of Fordean civilization on a mind unprepared for such an onslaught. Therefore his death significantly complicates the satirical direction of *Brave New World*, implicating both the irrational freedom of the Reservation as well as the oppressive regimentation of the World State. *Robert S. Baker, 1982*

d) *On the role of Shakespeare:*

1. *Brave New World* is constructed around an extended contrast of Shakespeare and H. G. Wells. Into the highly specialized society of the brave new world Huxley introduces the throw-back Savage, whose grasp of English and consequently of reality is based on repeated readings of Shakespeare's plays. [...] The allusive speech of the Savage produces a continual contrast between a total, imaginative view of life and the one-sided, incomplete, chiefly functional existences led by the inhabitants of a brave new world that Huxley intends as a satire on what he feels is H. G. Wells's misguided notion of utopia. [...] Shakespeare becomes and remains for Huxley the incarnation of the ideal, complete artist who sees the multiplicity of life.
Jerome Meckier, 1962

2. These references [to *Othello* and *King Lear*] are for the most part casual; they are more ornamental than functional; they display the author's ingenuity, but they cannot be said to constitute a pattern of sustained allusion. One play of Shakespeare's, however, *The Tempest*, bears a more intimate relationship to *Brave New World* than the others.
Ira Grushow, 1962

3. Later, when Lenina attempts to kiss John, he recalls this "feelie" [about the Negro and the blonde] with horror. [...] But the irony of the situation is that Huxley has made the "feelie" plot show us the Brave New World's version of *Othello*, and he has built his own plot on the outline of *Othello* as well. *William Jones, 1961*

Sources of quotes:

a) 1."Biology and Mr Huxley" in *Scrutiny*, May 1934; 2. *Huxley and Orwell*, London 1976, p.35; 3. *The Impact of Science on Society*, London 1952, pp.53-54 (1968 edition); 4. *Aldous Huxley*, London 1954, p.23; 5. *The Shape of Utopia*, Chicago 1970, p.89; b) 1. *Aldous Huxley, a Biography* London 1973, p.246; 2. "Women in Utopia" in *Alternative Futures*, vol.2, no 1 (1979), p.39; 3. *The Dark Historic Page*, London 1982, p.143; c) 1. "The Two Future Worlds of Aldous Huxley" in *PMLA* 77 (1962), p.329; 2. *Utopia and Anti-Utopia in Modern Times*, London 1987, p.287; 3. *The End of Utopia*, London 1984, p.49; 4. "Huxley and Lawrence" in *Virginia Quarterly Review* 13 (Autumn 1937), p.553; 4. as b) 3., p.142; d) 1. "Shakespeare and Aldous Huxley" in *Shakespeare Quarterly* vol.22 (1971); 2. *"Brave New World* and *The Tempest"* in *College English* 24, (October 1962), p.42; 3. "Western Humanities Review" no.15 (Summer 1961) p.276.

a) 1. **at large** as a whole, in general – **sardonic** mocking, full of irony – 2. **test-tube** *Retorte* – **faulty** defective, imperfect – **to distort** to change into an unnatural shape – **to tamper with** to change s.th. without permission – 3. **incompatible** [ɪŋkəm'pætəbl] unable to exist with s.th. else – **to perish** to be destroyed, to die – 4. **profitably** here: resulting in interesting insights – **the late** having recently died (Orwell died in 1950.) – 5. **to despair of** to have no hope of

b) 1. **life-span** the time that the average person lives – **dread** [dred] great fear – **the price** here: what has to be given up – **graduated** here: with fine differences and variations – **endurance** ability to suffer patiently, to undergo difficult times – **squalor** ['skwɒlə] (fig.) normally: a condition of being disgusting and full of dirt – 2. **to shudder** to tremble or shake with fear or horror – **to brood over** to watch over protectively – 3. **attributable to** considered to be caused by – **eradication** complete destruction – **repudiation** refusal to accept, rejection – **disavowal** [ˌdɪsə'vɒʊəl] disapproval, refusal to acknowledge – **dismissal** refusal to consider seriously – **historicist** [-'---] having to do with the belief that there are certain processes in history that man can do little to alter – **aversion** (usu.: ~ to) strong dislike

c) 1. **antagonist** person who is against s.th. – **to violate** here: to destroy – 2. **in the vein of** [veɪn] in the manner of – **prudish** ['pru:dɪʃ] easily shocked or upset about sexual matters – **disdain** complete lack of respect, contempt – **to pursue** to try to find – **the stuff of** (fig.) what s.th. is made of, substance – **debased** [dɪ'beɪst] made cheaper or of lower quality, corrupted, perverted – 3. **to exercise restraint** to hold back from doing s.th. – **lust** sexual desire – **hence...** this explains... – **on**

his own terms as he defines it – 4. **agonizing** causing great suffering and pain – 5. **to attribute to** to explain by – **pernicious** [pə'nɪʃəs] very harmful and destructive, evil – **onslaught** ['ɒnslɔ:t](fig.) violent attack – **to implicate** to put the blame on – **regimentation** very strict control over a group of people – **World State** i. e. Brave New World

d) 1. **extended** here: spread out over the novel – **throw-back** characteristic of an earlier or more primitive condition – **grasp** understanding, comprehension – **allusive** full of allusions (*Anspielungen*) – **incarnation** here: best example – **multiplicity** great variety – 2. **casual** done without much thought – **ingenuity** cleverness and originality – **to constitute** to form, to make up, to compose – **sustained** continuous, kept up through the novel – **to bear a relationship to** to relate to

Comparison with the German Translation

ERSTES KAPITEL

Ein grauer gedrungener Bau, nur vierunddreißig Stockwerke hoch. Über dem Haupteingang die Worte: BRUT- UND NORMZENTRALE BERLIN-DAHLEM. Darunter, auf einer Tafel, der Wahlspruch des Weltstaats: GEMEINSCHAFTLICHKEIT, EINHEITLICHKEIT, BESTÄNDIGKEIT.

Der riesige Saal zu ebener Erde ging nach Norden. Durch die Fenster drang spärlich Licht, kalt und hart trotz dem Sommer jenseits der Scheiben und der tropischen Hitze in dem Raum selbst, und suchte gierig irgendeine drapierte Gliederpuppe, den blassen Umriß eines fröstelnden Modells, fand aber nur das Glas und Nickel und frostig glänzende Porzellan eines Laboratoriums. Kälte stieß auf Kälte. Die Arbeiter trugen weiße Kittel, ihre Hände steckten in blassen, leichenfarbenen Gummihandschuhen. Das Licht war kalt, tot, gespenstisch. Nur von den gelben Tuben der Mikroskope lieh es sich eine gewisse lebendige Fülle und lag wie Butter auf den blanken Zylindern, ein satter Streif nach dem anderen, die endlose Reihe der Arbeitstische entlang.

„Und dies", sagte der Direktor, die Tür öffnend, „ist der Befruchtungsraum."

Dreihundert Befruchter standen über ihre Instrumente gebeugt, als der Brut- und Normdirektor den Saal betrat. Kaum ein Atemzug unterbrach die Stille, kaum ein gedankenverlorenes Vor-sich-hin-Summen oder -Pfeifen störte die allgemeine angespannte Vertieftheit. Eine soeben eingetroffene Gruppe sehr junger, sehr rosiger und sehr unerfahrener Studenten folgte aufgeregt und ein bißchen beklommen dem Direktor auf den Fersen. Jeder hielt ein Merkheft in der Hand, in das er, sooft der große Mann den Mund auftat, krampfhaft kritzelte. Aus erster Quelle – eine besondere Gunst. Der Brut- und Normdirektor von Berlin legte Wert darauf, seine neuen Studenten höchstpersönlich durch die einzelnen Abteilungen zu führen.

„Nur damit Sie eine Vorstellung vom Ganzen bekommen", erklärte er in solchen Fällen. Irgendeine Vorstellung mußten sie schließlich haben, wenn sie ihre Arbeit mit Verstand verrichten sollten, andererseits aber auch keine zu genaue Vorstellung, wenn sie brauchbare und zufriedene Mitglieder der Gesellschaft werden sollten. Die kleinen Einzelheiten sind es bekanntlich, die tüchtig und glücklich machen. Gesamtüberblicke sind für den Geist nur von Übel. Nicht Philosophen, sondern Hobbybastler und Briefmarkensammler bilden das Rückgrat der Menschheit.

„Morgen", setzte der BUND gewöhnlich hinzu und lächelte mit einem nicht ganz geheuren Wohlwollen, „beginnt für Sie der Ernst der Arbeit. Für Gesamtüberblicke werden Sie dann keine Zeit haben. Inzwischen..."

Inzwischen war es eine besondere Gunst: aus erster Quelle ins Merkheftchen. Die Jungen kritzelten wie besessen. Hochgewachsen und mager, aber stramm, schritt der Direktor allen voran in den Saal. Er hatte ein langes Kinn und große, ziemlich vorstehende Zähne, gerade noch von den vollen, üppig geschwungenen Lippen bedeckt, wenn er schwieg. Alt? Jung? Dreißig, fünfzig, fünfundfünfzig? Schwer zu sagen. Übrigens ergab sich die Frage gar nicht, denn in diesem Jahre der Beständigkeit, 632 n.F., fiel es niemandem ein, sie zu stellen.

1. How has the translator changed the setting? How might the translator have justified this change?
2. In the translation a number of names and place names have been changed. What are the pros and cons of taking such a liberty?
   Examples:
   Henry Forster – Henry Päppler/ John – Michel/ Bernard Marx – Sigmund Marx/ Mustafa Mond – Mustafa Mannesmann/ Gaffney (at Eton) – Nietzschlegel/ Lenina Crowne – Lenina Braun/ Fanny – Stinni/ Helmholz Watson – Helmholz Holmes-Watson/ Linda – Filine/ Fifi Bradlaugh – Monisma Haeckel/ Joanna Diesel – Drahtleite Diesel/ Clara Deterding – Marlene Deterding/ Herbert Bakunin – Valentino Bakunin/ Stoke Poges – Döberitz/ Bloomsbury – Dahlem/ Eton – Pforta/ Westminster Abbey – Berliner Dom
3. The translation was made in 1932; most modern translators would neither change the setting nor the names. Why?
4. How successfully are the words and expressions translated into German? What is lost in the translation?
   Compare in particular the following German translations with the original words and phrases:

Einheitlichkeit (l. 4)	Gruppe (l. 24)
frostig glänzende (l. 10)	beklommen (l. 25)
Kälte (l. 11)	Gesamtüberblicke (l. 37)
Fülle (l. 15)	Hobbybastler (l. 38)
satter (l. 16)	sagte...setzte.. gewöhnlich hinzu (l. 40)
...angespannt (l. 23)	nicht ganz geheuren (l. 41)

5. What is "... aus erster Quelle" a translation of? What gets lost in the translation? (Consider the description of the Director which follows.)
6. How are the present participle constructions translated into German? (Examples: "hungrily seeking..."; "but finding only the glass..."; "lying along the polished tubes..."; "opening the door"; "smiling at them...".)

7. Compare the passage “Bent...over their instruments...concentration.” with its translation.
8. How successfully does the translator reproduce the tone and atmosphere of the original?
9. There have been a number of translations for the title of the book. Which of the following do you find best? Explain.
   a) *Welt – wohin* (1932)
   b) *Wackere neue Welt* (1950)
   c) *Schöne neue Welt* (1981)

General Questions

1. Make a report about how various philosophers define happiness and compare with *Brave New World*. What is happiness for you?
2. What role do violence and sex play in the novel? Compare with Orwell’s *1984*.
3. How is the family seen in Brave New World? What seems to be Huxley’s opinion? Consider also his “good utopia”, *Island* (see pp. 95, 106).
4. Compare the role of literature and art in present-day society with Brave New World.
5. Reconstruct the past history of Brave New World. (There are references in Chapters 1, 2, 3, 16 and 17.)
6. To what extent does the past and human nature infiltrate Brave New World society? What is Huxley trying to say?
7. What inherent weaknesses are there in Brave New World that might lead to its downfall?
8. Read any or all of the “background texts” and say how they relate to *Brave New World*.
9. From what viewpoint is the story told? Why?
10. Who are the protagonists in the novel? In what way are they similiar to each other, and different? With which character do you most sympathize? Explain.
11. Who are the antagonists in the story? Characterize them.
12. Which characters are three-dimensional? Which are flat? Do any change or develop?
13. Determine the climax or climactic scenes.
14. In what way does the novel borrow techniques from film making?
15. What techniques of characterization does the author use?
16. Characterize the civilization of the Savage and that of Mustapha Mond. Are there any similarities between them? Which do you prefer? Why?
17. Compare Mond with O’Brien in Orwell’s *1984*.
18. Give examples of satire. What are the targets of this satire? How relevant is this satire to our own times? Consider religion, entertainment, death, sex, class structure, etc.
19. Discuss the role of Shakespeare in the novel.
20. Bearing in mind that Huxley’s novel was published in 1932, how many of his predictions have come true?
21. What moral predicaments are we faced with today because of scientific advances?

22. Make a report about the various schools of psychology. (Freud, Jung, Watson, Skinner, etc.). Which school appeals most to you? Why?
23. Try to explain man's constant striving to find a utopia.
24. Make up your own ideal state or utopia. Deal with sex, the family, education, science, art and literature.

List of Literary Terms

alliteration [-ˌ--ˈ--]	repetition of the same sound at the beginning of words close together; e.g. "I hear lake water lapping with low sounds by the shore" (W.B. Yeats)
allusion [-ˈ--]	an indirect reference to another work of literature, person, or event (*Anspielung*)
anaphora [əˈnæfərə]	repetition of a word or phrase at the beginning of successive clauses; e.g. "…we cannot dedicate, we cannot consecrate, we cannot hallow this ground…" (Abraham Lincoln)
antagonist [-ˈ---]	the character in a story or drama who is opposed to the hero/heroine (or protagonist)
antithesis [ænˈtɪθɪsɪs]	use of strongly contrasting words or phrases balanced grammatically against each other; e.g. "The richer we have become materially, the poorer we have become spiritually." (Martin Luther King)
characterization	1. the means used by an author to develop a character (e.g. by physical description, by presentation of the character's thoughts, by showing how others react, etc.) 2. the actual image of a character which is developed in the course of a story
climax	the point in a story or play when a crisis is reached and a resolution can be expected; often called the "turning point"
collage [-ˈ-]	(Fr.) a term first used to describe a painting technique which involved sticking together materials from different sources; can also describe a similar technique in literature
counterpoint	a musical term meaning the combination of two or more melodies; sometimes applied to a combination of different metres in poetry, or to a "collage" of different short scenes in a novel
dénouement [ˌdeɪˈnʊːmɑːŋ]	the outcome of the plot, the part of a play or story in which conflicts are resolved, mysteries or secrets are explained
diction	the choice and use of words in writing
euphemism [ˈjuːfɪˌmɪzəm]	a polite word or expression used to avoid talking about s.th. unpleasant; e.g. "to pass away" instead of "to die"

epigram ['epɪˌgræm] short, witty pointed statement in verse or prose; e.g. "Nothing is as dangerous as being too modern; one is apt to grow old-fashioned so suddenly." (Oscar Wilde)

exposition the part of a narrative or drama, usually at the beginning, in which important background information about the characters and events is given

farce [fɑ:s] a type of comedy based on a ridiculous situation often with stereotyped characters

foreshadowing hints or clues in a story or play that suggest what will happen later

hyperbole [haɪ'pɜ:bəlɪ] exaggeration; e.g. He kissed her a thousand times.

irony a deliberately created discrepancy between words and their intended meanings. There are two main kinds in literature: 1. verbal irony – when a character or the author/narrator says one thing and means s.th. completely different. 2. dramatic irony – when a character says or does s.th. without realizing its real significance, which is evident to the reader/audience.

litotes ['laɪtəʊˌtɪ:z] understatement; e.g. AIDS is no small problem.

memento mori (Lat.) any reminder of death, e.g. a skull

metaphor ['metəfə] a way of comparing two basically different things without using "as" or "like"; one thing is described in terms of the other; e.g. "…the milk of human kindness…" (Shakespeare)

metonymy [mɪ'tɒnɪmɪ] using an attribute to stand for s.th.; e.g. "the crown" to mean the monarch

montage [mɒn'tɑ:ʒ] (Fr.) in motion pictures: the rapid sequence of short scenes or images that show different aspects of the same idea or situation

narrator the person in whose words a story is told. It may be told in the author's own voice, or in an adopted voice. In either case, the narrator can remain outside the story (speaking in the third person) or be part of it (speaking also in the first person).

onomatopoeia [ˌɒnəˌmætə'pɪ:ə] word that imitates a sound; e.g. to hiss, to buzz

oxymoron [ˌɒksɪ'mɔ:rɒn] combination of seemingly contradictory words for a special effect; e.g. "I like a smuggler. He is the only honest thief." (Charles Lamb)

paradox ['pærəˌdɒks] a seemingly contradictory statement that on closer examination has some truth in it e.g. "Careless she is with artful care…" (William Congreve)

parody ['pærədɪ] the imitation of an author's words, style, attitude, and ideas in such a way as to make them look ridiculous

periphrasis [pəˈrɪfrəsɪs] — using a complicated way of writing or saying s.th. that could be expressed in simple words; e.g. The defender of society apprehended the fugitive from the law. i.e. The policeman arrested the criminal.

personification — giving human qualities to objects, e.g. "The waves beside them danced..." (William Wordsworth, in "The Daffodils")

plot — the sequence of events or actions in a work of literature

point of view — the way the narrator presents the characters and events in a story; e.g. a) as a first-person narrative, restricted to this speaker's point of view or b) as a third-person narrative, which can either be limited to one character's point of view, move freely between the points of view of different characters, as if the narrator were omniscient (all-knowing), or be limited to what can be seen and heard, i.e. no inner thoughts are given (camera-eye point of view)

polysyndeton [ˌpɒlɪˈsɪndɪtən] — repetition of the same conjunction, especially "and"; e.g. "She was beautiful and he loved to look at her and her feet felt very good on his." (Ernest Hemingway in "In a Strange Country")

protagonist [-ˈ---] — the main character in a work of literature on whom the action centers, the hero/heroine; opposite: antagonist

proverb [ˈprɒvɜːb] — a short saying that contains a general truth e.g. Early to bed, early to rise, makes a man healthy, wealthy, and wise. (Benjamin Franklin)

satire [ˈsætaɪə] — the use of sarcasm, wit, and irony to show the moral weakness of an individual, institution, or even society, e.g. George Orwell's *Animal Farm*

setting — the time and place of a story or drama, the physical background

simile [ˈsɪmɪlɪ] — a comparison using "as" or "like"; e.g. "My love is like a red, red rose..." (poem by Robert Burns) (cf. metaphor)

stock character — (also: stereotype) a character that appears so often in literature that his or her nature is immediately familiar to the reader; e.g. the absent-minded professor, the mad scientist, the all-knowing but silent butler

stream of consciousness — (also: interior monologue) a style of writing that attempts to imitate the natural flow of a character's thoughts, feelings, mental images, memories as the character experiences them; e.g. "My handkerchief. He threw it. I remember. Did I not take it up? His hand groped vainly in his pockets. No, I didn't. Better buy one." (James Joyce, in *Ulysses*)

style — choice and arrangement of words, sentence structure, use of figurative language, rhythm, and tone that determine a writer's form of expression

suspension of disbelief — the idea that a reader willingly accepts a certain lack of logic or reality in a work of literature, because it has a deeper truth to it (coined by Samuel Coleridge, 1772-1834)

symbol — anything that stands for s.th. else; e.g. the Cross as a symbol of Christianity

tragedy — a dramatic form in which events move to a fatal or disastrous conclusion. The downfall of the hero (usually resulting from a "tragic flaw" in his character in combination with forces beyond his control) arouses our pity.